Chariots of Fire

And a Christian Message for Today

Chariots of Fire

W. J. WEATHERBY

Based on a Screenplay by

COLIN WELLAND

And a Christian Message for Today

JIM AND ANNE RYUN

A QUICKSILVER BOOK

Harper & Row, Publishers, San Francisco

Cambridge, Hagerstown, New York, Philadelphia

London, Mexico City, São Paulo, Sydney

1817

FIRST HARPER & ROW EDITION PUBLISHED IN 1983

Designer: Jim Mennick

Library of Congress Cataloging in Publication Data

Weatherby, William J.
   CHARIOTS OF FIRE.

  "A Quicksilver book."
  1. Abrahams, Harold Maurice, 1899–   —Fiction. 2. Liddell, Eric, 1902–1945—Fiction. I. Welland, Colin. II. Ryun, Jim, 1947– . III. Ryun, Anne. IV. Title.
V. Title: Christian message for today.
PR6073.E13C5   1983   823'.914   82–48941
ISBN 0–06–069282–0

---

83 84 85 86 87 10 9 8 7 6 5 4 3 2 1

Contents

Publisher's Introduction

Continuing a tradition whose recorded history extends to 776 B.C., the Olympics demonstrate the connection between physical stamina and mental and spiritual determination. The location of the original games illustrates this point: site of the sacred grove of Zeus, the supreme deity, and the Temple of Hera, the goddess of war, Olympia was located in western Greece, on a broad, fertile plain ten miles from the sea. Nestled in the confluence of two rivers, it was a center for religious ceremonies as well as a showplace for physical prowess.

This edition of *Chariots of Fire* reverberates with the countless footfalls of Olympic heroes, men and women who became legends in their own time. Eric Liddell, Harold Abrahams, and Jim Ryun, the personalities represented in this volume, typify the mythic struggle required of each participant in the Olympic games.

All Olympians must wrestle with both inherited and developed qualities—physical abilities, mental and moral stamina, psychological temperament, ethnic pride, and religious conviction—as they persevere to experience and champion the great race of life.

Jim and Anne Ryun know all about "running the race"—both on the track and in the game of life. Jim became an international track figure while yet in high school, competing in the 1964 Olympics as a seventeen-year-old. He went on to establish world records in middle distances, including the 1500 meters and the mile. But his career was not without defeat: he was bested by altitude in the 1968 Olympics in Mexico City, and his spill on the track at the 1972 Olympics in Munich is well known.

Through it all his wife, Anne, has stood by Jim, helping him weather the fickleness of fans and the pressure of the press. It is out of the crucible of their life together, their knowledge of victory and defeat, that they now bring their particular Christian vision and insight to inform this commentary on the text of *Chariots of Fire.*

1

Running a race hasn't changed much in a thousand years. It is still a supreme test of the individual. When the starter's pistol cracks, runners are alone, dependent on themselves. The greater their physical and mental conditioning, the greater the runners. The immortals of the track become "chariots of fire," driven by a burning desire to win.

This is the story of two great "chariots of fire" — Harold Abrahams and Eric Liddell. They lived not long ago, but their story has the timeless quality of an ancient legend. Like mythical heroes, they set themselves a supreme task — to become the fastest men on earth. Each of them triumphed in his own way.

Harold Abrahams turned himself into a "chariot of fire" with scientific thoroughness, carefully analyzing and correcting his errors, whereas Eric Liddell achieved his peak by breaking all the rules, running as naturally as a wild animal.

They made a perfect contrast, like a scientist matched

with an artist, but they had in common an unbeatable drive, mined from their deepest personal resources.

Harold Abrahams' obsession with winning was strongly influenced by his status as the son of a German Jew, forced to battle prejudice in an English society that treated him as an alien. His running triumphs were intended to enforce his acceptance as a native son, the equal of anybody.

Eric Liddell, a Scottish missionary's offspring, had no such identity problems, but found his inspiration from his religious beliefs, racing for the glory of God and refusing to compromise even in the Olympic Games.

Both men won gold medals in the Olympics of 1924. The Olympic ideal at that time had not yet begun to crack under the strain of international politics. Winning a race in the Olympics was still considered an individual triumph. So riding their "chariots of fire," Harold Abrahams and Eric Liddell were able to win on their own terms. Their characters were much more important to their running than any outside influences.

Perhaps they can inspire young men and women the world over to rekindle the Olympic torch before competition between nations and political expedience snuff out the ideal of individual contests forever.

That is why their story deserves to be told again.

Everyone Who Hears These Words

Every one then who hears these words of mine and does them will be like a wise man who built his house upon the rock; and the rain fell, and the floods came, and the winds blew and beat upon that house, but it did not fall, because it had been founded on the rock. And every one who hears these words of mine and does not do them will be like a foolish man who built his house upon the sand; and the rain fell, and the floods came, and the winds blew and beat against that house, and it fell; and great was the fall of it.

Matthew 7:24–27, RSV

Running today draws thousands and interests millions. A classic struggle of one human being against another (and a visionary picture of life), its appeal has increased over the years. The characteristics of any runner are not dissimilar to those of our two main characters—and of any one of us who is about to enter into this true life story. The contrast between Eric Liddell and Harold Abrahams is certainly intriguing. We see a picture of God's creative versatility in these two men—one so intense, the other so trusting that the Lord has everything under control.

This story will hold you in the balance between

these two strikingly different personalities. You will see yourself clearly in Harold—the inner drive and desire to attain, acquire, and succeed. Then you will see your hopes in Eric—how you want your life to be lived, loving your Lord, your Creator, with all your heart, mind, and soul. You will see how to live the word of God so naturally that it is indeed a lifestyle—one to be integrated into every bone and breath of your being.

In this, as in every story, there are contributing characters who help to mold and shape and influence who we are and who we want to become. Listen and watch how they affect Harold's and Eric's lives and help to make them the men they are. This is certainly a story that needs to be told again and again. Let us not let it die with Eric and Harold, but let us tell it again living out our lives to the glory of our Lord.

Questions for Reflection and Discussion

1. The 1924 Olympics came on the heels of World War I. That time in history was one of rebuilding and restoring lives, as well as entire nations. How did the war's influence help shape Eric and Harold? How do the world's happenings help shape our lives and destinies as Christians today?
2. Who are the contributing characters in your life? Tell how they have affected you for better or worse.
3. Have people influenced you from attaining your goals or detained you from fulfilling your aspirations?
4. There is a challenge in this story. Whose life would you most like yours to be like—Eric's or Harold's?

2

Cambridge, England—1919.

World War One, the "Great War" to end all wars, was just over. Millions of young men—the so-called "Lost Generation"—had been killed in the four bloody years of trench warfare in France. Their shadows lay across the post-war world. A settled, secure way of life in Europe had been destroyed. Now the way was clear for great changes, bringing opportunities to people who had been denied a chance until the German guns made so many vacancies in the seats of power.

Young Harold Abrahams hoped to be one of these people. A brilliant student, a fine athlete with the makings of a great sprinter, he had all the qualities needed for success in English society except the right Anglo-Saxon Protestant upper class breeding. He was a Jew, and he was convinced this branded him an outsider and excluded him from any share in the running of the country—until the war did its terrible work and wiped out so many of the future elite. The pattern of English society was shaken up forever, and young Harold saw his chance to win recognition. And where better to do it than at Cambridge University, where so many of the rulers of England had been educated?

The first post-war freshmen had already begun to arrive at Cambridge, flooding into the ancient university town by every train, loaded with their personal possessions and hiding their feelings under a great deal of bravado.

Harold was among them, but even then he stood out in a crowd. Tall and dark-haired, with tanned skin and flashing eyes, a mature twenty-year-old, he was already a formidable personality, much more self-confident than most of the arriving freshmen. He was aggressive, articulate and quick to take offense.

Stepping off the train from London, he looked for a porter to help him with his luggage. At last he saw one and called the man over, but he was ignored. This happened a second time. Harold strode angrily over to the station master to complain.

A fat little man in a formal railway uniform, the station master tried to explain that it was the result of the war—there was a general shortage of porters—but Harold cut in. The war was no excuse, he snapped. The war was over, but in his mind, Harold was always fighting his private war against prejudice.

He grabbed his bags and hurried away down the crowded station platform, blind to everything except his own hurt feelings. He narrowly missed one student and then collided with another, who was heavily laden with suitcases, tennis rackets, and golf clubs.

"I'm terribly sorry," Harold apologized, suddenly all charm and smiles. "Look, I've an arm free. Let me carry your golf clubs. I see you're quite a sportsman," he added cheerfully.

"All show really," remarked the other young man, who introduced himself as Aubrey Montague. "I take it you're not keen on sport."

"I run," Harold replied firmly.

"Really?" Aubrey was tall and broad-shouldered, but with a gentle look that made Harold trust him at once. "I run, too. Only trouble is I can't stand getting beaten. How about you?"

Harold gave one of his flashing smiles that seemed arrogant to some people.

"I don't know. I've never lost."

It wasn't said boastfully, but as a quiet statement of fact. It showed a rather un-English self-assurance, Aubrey Montague thought, studying his new friend. Was he so confident because he was Jewish and had to assert himself? Aubrey had no time to think about the answer because Harold was already staggering into the street under the weight of their belongings. A man in his early twenties, with a much older face and ragged clothes, offered to help Harold.

"Carry your bags, sir? Find you a taxi?"

"No, thanks," said Harold. Then he noticed the war medals pinned to the young man's coat and his missing arm. This was one of the survivors of the war, a maimed veteran. One of the working class who had taken a bad beating in the trenches, he now had to hustle a living any way he could. He felt a deep hostility for the two young

7

students in their expensive tweed suits, with their privileges and elitist future, but he didn't let it show as he tried to profit from any guilt feelings they might have about his war wounds. He had nearly thrust his empty sleeve under Harold's nose. It paid off. Harold let him carry a bag to a taxi and gave him a generous tip. Luckily Harold didn't see the man bite the coin and then spit on the road, or hear him say to another war veteran as the taxi sped away, "That's what we fought the bloody war for—to give all the Jew boys a proper education." Anti-semitism was as strong among the working class as the upper class; that wouldn't have surprised Harold. But he would have felt bad that a man who had lost an arm and experienced so much of the war had learned so little.

Cambridge seemed to be full of bicycles. The taxi-driver was continually honking his horn to clear a way. The two young students gazed out at their new home. At first sight, except for its bicycles, Cambridge was almost too drenched in history, even the most modern buildings somehow being touched by the styles of other periods.

When the taxi stopped outside Caius* College, the two students surveyed the carved coat of arms over the arched entrance. Aubrey had a respectful expression, but Harold hadn't come to revere the past; his mind was on conquering the present.

---

*pronounced *Cays*.

8

They paid the taxi-driver and carried their luggage into an inner quadrangle, where the noise of the street was shut out. Harold stared moodily at the trim lawn surrounded by medieval arches.

"Penny for your thoughts?" said Aubrey.

"I was thinking about my parents, that's all," Harold replied abruptly. This would all seem so foreign to them, he thought, but they wanted him to be a part of it.

A deep voice growled from the porter's lodge, a little reception office just beyond the main entrance to the college, "In here, gentlemen, if you please."

The head porter confronted them in top hat and tails. His assistant by his side was dressed in mere morning clothes and bowler hat. These men assigned the students to their rooms and helped to look after their needs, never quite sure whether they were servants or supervisors, their manner a mixture of polite condescension and veiled hostility.

"Names please," grunted the head porter, a heavily built man with a thin mustache.

"We're new," Harold replied evenly.

"I can see that, laddy. Name?"

Harold quietly gave his name. The head porter glanced up and Harold recognized his expression—it was the moment when someone recognized you as a Jew.

"Which school?" The head porter consulted his list. "Repton—that the one?"

"That's it. I left a year ago."

"Been doing your bit in the army, have you? France?"

"No . . . joined too late."

"Bad luck, lad."

"There's many a man would have liked a share of it— bad or not."

The head porter eyed him silently, with dislike.

Harold took the offensive.

"What are your names?"

"Rogers. I'm head porter. And this is Mr. Ratcliffe, my assistant."

"Well, Mr. Rogers, Ratcliffe, I ceased to be called 'laddy' when I took up the King's Commission. Is that clear?"

The head porter nodded coldly.

"Yes, Mr. Abrahams, quite clear."

"Thank you. I'd be obliged if you'd remember it." He gave Aubrey a friendly nod, pleased with himself for having set the head porter straight. "Meet up with you later," he told his new friend as he strode away to find the room assigned to him.

"What's your friend studying?" asked the head porter. "Barrack room law?"

"I've no idea," said Aubrey.

"Well, one thing's certain, with a name like Abrahams, he won't be in the chapel choir, will he?"

Aubrey could see the malice in the man's eyes and didn't reply. He was beginning to understand Harold's aggressive attitude—strike before they strike you. Would he ever be fully accepted at Cambridge? What had he said about his running? *I've never lost.* Perhaps that applied to his life, too.

Aubrey Montague soon learned more about his new friend. Harold Abrahams was the son of a Jewish financier, who had emigrated to London from Germany. He was very conscious of his Jewishness, for clearly few in this newly adopted land would let him forget it, and he felt a desperate need to carve a niche for himself in the ruling circles of his father's chosen country. He was defensive, ambitious, and yet, Aubrey soon discovered, also warm-hearted and generous.

He couldn't have been more different from Aubrey himself, the loyal son of gentle southern English middle-class parents, who dreamed of becoming a great journalist. But they became fast friends. Their mutual passion for running helped. Aubrey knew as soon as he watched Harold sprint a hundred yards that he was destined to be a great runner, perhaps the fastest of his time. Harold had the physique, the stamina, the speed, and a serious attention to detail in training that Aubrey had never seen before in such a young athlete, but above all he had the drive and right mental attitude. His fast start was the result of long practice and deep concentration, and he was always able to find the energy for a final burst of speed that took him ahead of Aubrey and the others. He seemed to come fully alive in a race, all his passionate feelings coming together in one fiery aim—to win. It seemed as if that volcano of pent-up resentment that was always smoldering in his personality finally erupted in the burst of speed that shot him ahead to the tape.

The two friends attended the Freshers' dinner together, a sumptuous candlelit occasion in the ancient timber-roofed Great Hall of Caius College. It was very formal,

11

with everyone in tuxedos. The atmosphere was almost churchlike, befitting a solemn ritual of the college.

Here they were introduced to their new status—as the new elite, the pick of England, the successors of the "Lost Generation." Behind the Master of the college was a tablet commemorating the students killed in the war. The Master's voice trembled with emotion as he called the dead Caius men by name, adding slowly, "They died to save England and all that England stands for."

He paused for a moment to control his feelings, and his young audience—fresh, clean, uniformly dressed in stiff white shirts and black ties—bowed their heads.

Aubrey glanced at Harold's expressionless face. His dark eyes were fixed on the Master as the old man continued, "And to you gentlemen, the new generation, have been bequeathed the hopes and dreams of those who went before you. Through tragic necessity their aspirations have become yours."

Most of the freshmen were quietly attentive with polite, respectful expressions, but Harold suddenly sat forward with that intense, challenging look that Aubrey had seen on the running track before the start of each race.

"I exhort you to examine yourselves," the Master was saying. "Assess your true potential, seek to discover where your true chance of greatness lies. . . . "

Harold's eyes seemed to glint confidently as if he knew already where *his* chance of greatness was to be found.

" . . . Seize your chance, rejoice in it and let no power nor persuasion deter you from your task."

Harold half-smiled. *Nothing* would deter him.

Watching him, Aubrey was impressed again by Harold's force of character; he seemed to stand out from the other freshmen with his passionate feelings and expressive looks and gestures. He was certainly a pretty remarkable chap, Aubrey decided. It wasn't only his great running potential. He took part in so many of the college's other activities. He seemed to be out to prove himself more "the pick of England" than anyone. He even joined in the college's amateur theatricals, performing in productions of the popular Gilbert and Sullivan comic operettas with great gusto. Aubrey sometimes suspected he was daring any other Englishman to think of him as different. When he sat at a piano accompanying himself in a Gilbert and Sullivan song, Harold seemed to be saying, "Look, you Anglo-Saxons, I'm more English than any of you."

But that was the public Harold Abrahams; in time, Aubrey was trusted enough to see the other private, brooding side. Late one night, over mugs of hot cocoa in Harold's room, Aubrey raised the sensitive subject of anti-semitism.

Harold stared thoughtfully into his mug. How did he feel about it? "Is that what you want to know, Aubrey? Well, I can tell you this. It's an ache, a helplessness, an anger." His voice rose impatiently. "One feels humiliated. Sometimes I say to myself—hey, steady on. You're imagining all this. And then I catch that look again, catch it on the edge of a remark, feel a cold reluctance in a handshake. . . . "

Harold's face was much more open and vulnerable than Aubrey had ever seen it. His defenses were down for once and his deepest feelings were clearly visible in his hurt look.

"My father—he's a German Jew, so he *is* alien." He smiled, trying to hide his feelings. "Spiritually, culturally, linguistically, and gastronomically, he's as foreign as a frankfurter."

"And a kosher one at that," added Aubrey with a smile, encouraging Harold to go on. He obviously needed to talk to someone or he would explode.

"I love and admire him. He worships this country. From nothing he built what he believed was enough to make true Englishmen of his sons." Harold rose and took from the mantel above the old fireplace a framed photograph of his family. "My brother's a doctor, a leader in his field," he said, showing Aubrey the photograph. "He wanted for nothing. And here am I setting up shop in the finest university in the land." His eyes flashed scornfully. "But the old man forgot one thing. This England of his is Christian and Anglo-Saxon . . . and so are her halls of intellect, her corridors of power. And those who would walk them guard them with jealousy and venom."

Aubrey chuckled.

"You're right to read law, Harold. You're quite an advocate."

"It's one of our rare ethnic advantages. It's called the gift of the gab." Harold smiled and added slowly, "Strangely enough, I've never consciously felt Jewish. Not even at school. And there they treated me like some rare species of ape. But this place—look at it. Every stone reeks of Anglican pomp and complacency. It's enough to de-convert St. Paul. I want to stand and cry out, and bring the whole damn place tumbling down."

"So what now?" asked Aubrey quietly. "Grin and bear it?"

Harold shook his head and said fiercely, "I'm going to take them on. One by one. *All* of them.

"*And run them off their feet!*"

In the weeks that followed, Harold's attitude became clearer when he decided to challenge for the Trinity Court Dash. This was a traditional race against the clock that had never been won in 700 years. The challenger had to run around the great lawn of Trinity Court while the Trinity clock struck mid-day. The distance was 312 paces, roughly 400 yards to be run in under a minute.

Harold's challenge at once made his name well-known. Students pointed him out in the street. With his usual dedication to detail, he studied the course round the great lawn. The ground was uneven, the corners sharp. It seemed a hopeless task, but Harold prepared with quiet confidence. This was his first attempt "to take them on," and he had never lost in his life.

He arrived in a topcoat over his running clothes, a scarf around his neck. He had a studied casualness typical of the university's style. Already hundreds of students were gathering around the edges of the lawn to witness Harold's assault on tradition. They were excited by his courage and effrontery. Some obtained grandstand views by positioning themselves at the mullioned windows

15

above the cloisters. Aubrey helped to clear a way for Harold so he could take the traditional position under the clock.

"What have you got on your feet, Abrahams?" someone shouted. "Rockets?"

It was 11:55. Five minutes to go. Harold had to begin on the clock's first strike and return before the strike of twelve. Voices yelled at him to go home, it was impossible. Others tried to encourage him. "You show 'em, Harold!" "Do it for Israel!"

Harold knew his only chance lay in the slow strike of the Trinity clock. It struck twice for each hour or twenty-four chimes for twelve o'clock. That allowed a little more time for covering the distance. But it still seemed impossible.

Watching from one of the windows, the Master of Trinity sipped a glass of sherry and discussed Harold Abrahams' impudence with the Master of Caius.

"This Abrahams. What do you know about him?"

"Repton chap," replied the Master of Caius. "Jewish. His father's a financier in the city."

"Financier? A euphemism for what, I wonder."

"I suspect he lends money."

"Exactly. And what did Repton have to say about his son?"

"Academically sound," said the Master of Caius. "Arrogant and defensive to the point of pugnacity."

"They invariably are."

"Yet possessing a keen sense of duty and loyalty."

The Master of Trinity frowned doubtfully. He looked down on the crowded court.

"Did they say he can run?"

"Like the wind!"

For all their superior feelings, the two old dons couldn't resist opening the window to get a better view.

Harold had taken off his topcoat and was ready. It was one minute to twelve. A chalk line marked the start. Spectators were asked to stand back. The crowd quietened as Harold toed the chalk line to find the best grip for a fast start.

The starter, a solemn young student, announced: "Owing to the absence of any other challenger, Mr. Abrahams will run alone."

Suddenly a voice shouted: "Not so, Mr. Starter!"

All heads turned to see who was pushing his way through the crowd. It was Andrew Lindsay, a wealthy young aristocrat well known for his carefree style and interest in sports. Lord Andrew, the sixteenth Earl of Cumbria, was the sort of upper class Englishman Harold expected to snub him.

With a flamboyant gesture, the handsome young Lord took off his topcoat revealing running clothes underneath. Tucked under one arm was a bottle of champagne. He tossed the bottle to Aubrey Montague as the starter demanded, "Your name and college if you please, sir."

"Lindsay. I race beside my friend here. We challenge the Trinity Court in the name of our schools and college—Repton, Eton and Caius." He shook Harold's hand and said with a grin, "Chap told me about this shindig over breakfast. I thought I might help push you along a bit."

Harold, who had expected some snobbish putdown,

warmed to Lindsay's obvious charm and friendliness. "I'm delighted," he said, eyeing the clock. "Good luck."

"Gentlemen," cried the starter, "To your marks, if you please."

Harold and Lord Andrew dropped to semi-crouch positions. The crowd was suddenly quiet as the clock's minute hand moved slowly towards twelve.

The opening chime began.

Heads looked up.

Then the clock struck one and the two runners were off in a lightning start.

The crowd roared as they raced for the first corner.

Harold was a yard ahead and increased his lead down the western side over uneven paving stones. At the second corner, he slipped over a worn stone and Lord Andrew caught up on the inside and stretched his long legs down the southern side. But Harold quickly recovered and the two men—Harold so dark and determined, the young Lord fair-haired and carefree—ran almost neck-and-neck.

The clock struck on . . . and on. Could they possibly complete the course in time?

Both men were gasping for breath at the third bend and slid into the last of the long straights, the eastern edge of the court.

Eleven strikes left!

The young Lord struggled to retain his slight lead, but Harold's finely disciplined body pushed ahead, and there was only a yard between them as they neared the final corner.

The crowd's excitement rose. The two runners clearly had a chance of beating the clock.

Skidding around the final bend, Lord Andrew had little energy left, but Harold found a finishing burst from somewhere within himself. Watching him, Aubrey Montague saw in the fury of his final effort the astonishing will to win he had sensed in his friend.

"Nineteen! Twenty! Twenty-one! . . . "

The crowd chanted out the count as Harold flung himself toward the finishing line.

"Twenty-two! Twenty-three! . . . "

He was over the line and into the waiting arms of Aubrey.

He had done it!

The exhausted young Lord followed five yards behind and collapsed over the line.

Harold, his topcoat round his shoulders, helped him to his feet—they were Harold and Andy to each other now, the race had made them friends for life. The crowd cheered them both. The champagne bottle popped open with a great gush and both runners took a long drink. Harold shook Andy's hand gratefully. Competition always helped him to run faster. Then he waved the champagne bottle at the crowd. Once more he was the hearty good fellow, the role he usually played with his fellow students. But Aubrey couldn't forget the fury of his final effort, his whole body and mind concentrated on one desperate aim—to beat the clock. Was that the real Harold? And what would happen to him if he ever lost?

Above the two runners, the Master of Trinity closed

the window, shutting out the cheers.

"Did they both do it?" inquired the Master of Caius, sipping his sherry.

"I think not. Young Lindsay failed by a whisker."

"A pity."

"It's been done—and by a Caius man. You must be very proud."

"I am. Of course I am. It's just . . . " The Master of Caius hesitated to express his true feelings.

"You'd have preferred he were an Englishman. Well, Hebrew or not, we've just witnessed an historic feat. One man in seven hundred years. Perhaps they *are* God's chosen people after all." He raised his sherry glass. "To Abrahams!" He stared down at Harold, intense and unsmiling, moving slowly through the back-slapping crowd. "I doubt if there's a swifter man in the Kingdom."

But he was wrong.

Fearfully and Wonderfully Made

> For you created my inmost being;
> > you knit me together in my mother's womb.
> I praise you because I am fearfully and wonderfully made;
> > your works are wonderful,
> > I know that full well.
> My frame was not hidden from you
> > when I was made in the secret place.
> When I was woven together in the depths of the earth,
> > your eyes saw my unformed body.
> All the days ordained for me
> > were written in your book
> > before one of them came to be.
> How precious to me are your thoughts, O God.
> > How vast is the sum of them.
> Were I to count them,
> > they would outnumber the grains of sand.
> When I awake,
> > I am still with you.
>
> Psalm 139:13–18, NIV

How well the Lord God of this universe knows each one of us, and loves us. He has known everything about us even before we were born. And, of course, God is God, making no mistake in the creation of each of us. He knows your frame, your outward physical makeup, and your inward being—your thoughts, desires, habits, temperament, and personality.

We first see Harold Abrahams as a young, brash, immature freshman, beginning to make his mark at Cambridge University. He projects an obvious front of self-confidence, which he feels is necessary to survive in an Anglo-Saxon environment. Behind this front lies an inner anger that causes him to fight for his identity. During his registration with the head porter at Caius College, it is apparent that he feels like a potential target for persecution.

Although he maintains a self-confident or arrogant

attitude, there is in him, as in each of us, a genuine need to be loved. Harold's guard is temporarily lowered when he finds in Aubrey Montague a friend who is willing to listen and understand. In Aubrey, Harold finds a confidant who will not use him for personal gain, and who accepts him as he is.

This acceptance is increasingly important as Harold's compelling determination to succeed and to excel above all others in all arenas of life grows during his college years. In areas where others have yet to dare, we find Harold eager for a challenge; his successful attempt in the 400-yard dash around the school courtyard, for example, was a feat that had not been achieved in 700 years.

Why is there in Harold this need to succeed? Who planted the seed? Is it due to his Jewish heritage? Did his family expect him to succeed continually? Was he a self-made man determined to have his way and to succeed at all costs? Or were these seeds planted by an omniscient God who knows our frame all too well? Or is this need to excel there because he has not allowed his identity and purpose for living to be fulfilled by a living God? Is it the result of a flawed relationship with God that could be resolved by realizing that God knows who he is and loves him?

I had always thought my identity was that of a world-class runner. In establishing world records in the 880 yards, the 1500 meters, and the one-mile run, I thought I would not only have the identity I desired, but also the acceptance I yearned for from others. Once those marks were achieved, however, the emptiness inside me remained. I came to recognize that

God's true love was not dependent on what I willfully accomplished, but on who I am, in Him. Without this knowledge of God's love for me, my identity was based on what I did and how well I did it. This is a human, not divine, concept of greatness. I am great in God's eyes because I have chosen to be one of his sons.

Harold often felt pushed into a position of action by others with whom he came in contact. Sometimes these encounters brought out his warmth, other times a cold, cutting temperament. To the head porter, Harold was openly and defiantly defensive. With Aubrey, on the other hand, Harold exhibited a compassionate warmth. He displayed a sincere desire for friendship.

Questions for Reflection and Discussion

1. How much latitude do you give a person at your first meeting? Do you close or encourage a relationship according to your choice of words and your attitude?
2. Harold often seemed uncompassionate to the point of arrogance. He felt a need to be always on the offensive so that people would not take advantage of him. When you meet people like Harold, are you offended to the point of lashing back at their arrogance, or are you challenged to understand and to help them?
3. There was a great contrast between the public Harold Abrahams and the private Harold Abrahams. Are your public and private selves in such opposition? If so, why are they? Should they be? Our lives

as Christians are not to be hidden behind closed doors or under bushels. We are the fifth gospel, a living example of Jesus Christ.

4. What causes the innate anger we feel in Harold? Is he a man without room for peace, a man totally at unrest, ill at ease with who he is? Is this so in your life? How might God's love heal those frustrations and give release from anger?

5. Harold possesses that wonderful trait of singleness of mind and purpose. He is dedicated to becoming the gold medalist at 100 meters in the Olympic Games—the best in the world at that distance. His clarity of action puts his mind, his body, and his spirit in unison. Is your life lived with this singleness of purpose, or is it confused by superficial distractions? What is God's purpose for your life?

3

Far from Cambridge in the Scottish Highlands, a fair-haired young man was the star attraction at a May Day Gathering, a traditional folk festival of music, dance and physical prowess.

The young man was Eric Liddell, a science student at Edinburgh University and already famous as a Scottish rugby player. Eric had been born in China, where his father was a missionary, but he had come to Scotland for his education. His ambition was to be a missionary, too, but because of the great speed he had displayed in his rugby playing, admirers were urging him to train seriously as a runner and race for Scotland in international competition.

As soon as he arrived at the May Day Gathering in the beautiful green Highlands, a mountainous range in the far north of Scotland, Eric was surrounded by admiring children asking for his autograph. He obliged them all with a good-natured modesty, giving special attention to each child. Behind him, bagpipes sounded across the grassy slopes, and Highland dancers performed with loud cries over traditional crossed swords laid out on the grass.

Watching Eric with anxious eyes was a young woman in her late teens. This was his sister, Jennie, whose shy, serious face looked out of place among the noisy, laughing Highland crowd. Jennie was worried that Eric's growing sporting fame would interfere with his true life's work — the mission of bringing God's word to the world. She especially disapproved of his ruddy-faced, red-haired university friend, Sandy McGrath, who acted as Eric's unofficial trainer. He wanted Eric to run in the final race of the May Day Gathering.

She told him sharply, "Do you not think the boy's got enough on his plate without taking up racing?"

"I'm asking him to have a go, that's all," Sandy McGrath replied patiently.

"Sandy, you know Eric as well as I do. He can't crack his egg in the morning without putting his back into it." Jennie watched Eric chatting to a group of his young admirers. "He's to get his degree, play his rugby, and work for the mission. There's no breath in the poor man for any more."

"But he's fast, Jennie, really fast," Sandy McGrath protested. "You can't deny him the chance. Get your brother on a track with a wee piece of technique and wonders will happen."

"Eric's special to me now, Sandy. Precious . . . as he is. I don't want him spoilt with all this running talk."

Sandy, a big, good-humored fellow, kept silent. He had been through this before with Jennie, who acted more like Eric's wife or mother than a sister. She wouldn't listen to his arguments. But he continued to insist Eric *must* run, even if Jennie became angry. Eric had a rare and wonderful gift and he mustn't squander it.

They both watched Eric presenting the prizes to the winners in the children's races. He had been asked also to make a speech. He stared down at his feet, his hands clasped behind him, as if preparing what he was about to say, and then in a quiet firm voice, he spoke directly to the crowd of men and women assembled on the grassy slope in front of him.

"When we're in China," he said, "my father often waxes lyrical about the beauties of his 'wee home in the glen.'"

The crowd of Highlanders beamed.

"Being oriental-born myself," he went on with a smile, "I suffer from a natural incredulity. And yet, looking about me now, at the heather and the hills, I can see that I was wrong. It *is* special."

He had won his audience. There was scattered applause and cries of "Hear, hear!"

"Thank you for welcoming our family home," Eric added, "and for reminding me that I am, and will be whilst I breathe, a *Scot*."

The applause was loud and prolonged. Sandy McGrath seized his opportunity.

"Before you allow Eric to go," he cried, "persuade him to run in the 200 yards open handicap so we can all see his great speed."

Jennie gave Sandy an angry look, but he ignored her as the crowd cheered. Eric noticed Jennie's reaction and hesitated for a moment. The cheering went on. Everyone wanted to see that incredible speed they had all heard about. Finally Eric glanced sadly at Jennie, knowing she wouldn't understand, and agreed to run.

The local runners were already lined up, waiting. Eric quietly undid his tie and took off his tweed jacket, and prepared to run in his shirt and trousers. He looked the complete amateur, giving the other runners an encouraging smile and waving to Jennie, who turned her face away.

The starter's pistol went off with a loud bang in the mountain air. At first Eric was lost in the crowd of runners. But then he suddenly appeared from behind, surging ahead with an incredible burst of speed. There were cries of astonishment from the crowd. Eric did everything wrong—his feet came up too high, his arms pumped wildly at shoulder level, his head was far back—but none of his mistakes mattered. He passed the leading runners with ease and went into a great final sprint, his head thrust back on his shoulders, his arms whirling. It was a breathtaking display of sheer power, as natural as a wild horse's gallop, and the crowd roared its admiration long before Eric passed the finishing line.

Sandy McGrath hurried to congratulate him, but Jennie walked quickly away, her head down.

The next day was a Sunday—the Sabbath—and Eric's father preached a rousing sermon in a local church. "The Kingdom of God is not a democracy," cried the Reverend James Dunlop Liddell in his Scottish accent. "There is no discussion, no deliberation, no referenda as to which way to go, which road to take. There is no low road, only the high . . . one right, one wrong, one voice . . . one absolute ruler . . . one benevolent despot, demanding to be obeyed. . . .''

Eric sat in the front pew, directly below the pulpit, listening again to the ideas and philosophy that had shaped his life. He never took his eyes off his father. This was the kind of man he wanted to be.

"Compromise is the language of the Devil," cried his father. "Only obey and ye shall be repaid in creation's most powerful coinage, the love of God. 'Love divine all love's excelling—pure unbounded love thou art!' Seek ye the Lord, bow down before him, and be exalted beyond your wildest dreams."

Eric felt Jennie watching him. He had to convince her there was nothing to worry about. His running was as much a part of him as his prayers.

When the service was over and the congregation came pouring out, two small boys began to kick a soccer ball across the road.

"D'ya not know what day it is?" Eric called to them.

"Aye, it's Sunday," one of the boys said respectfully, for Eric was a hero after his race the day before.

"It is, right enough," replied Eric. "And the Sabbath's not a day for football, is it?"

The boy shook his head.

"Are you up early in the morning?" Eric asked gently.

"Aye, me Ma gets me up at seven."

"We'll have a game then. Are you on?"

"Aye, Mr. Liddell. Thanks. Can I bring ma Dad?"

Eric laughed. "Sure you can. Bring the whole family. And I'll give you five goals start."

The boy shouted the news to his friend.

Jennie said quickly, "Eric, you'll have no time. We've a train to catch at nine."

"We've to make time," he told her. "The kid's got to fear God, Jennie, but not think He's a spoilsport."

Jennie frowned with annoyance, but didn't express her true feelings until the family had dinner that night in their rented rooms. Big framed photographs of Eric's rugby triumphs and of the whole family at the mission house in China covered the walls as if the memories they evoked helped to transform the plain rented rooms into a real home.

Over dinner, Sandy McGrath proposed a toast to Eric's father and mother who were shortly returning to China, leaving Eric and Jennie behind to complete their education.

"Bon voyage, a safe journey back," said Sandy, "and may the years ahead in China be happy, blissful, content and blessed. To those who remain behind, may God protect them, inspire them"—he paused for a moment, staring across the table at Eric—"and lead them to Glory."

While Jennie glared at him, her mother said, "Thank you, Sandy. That was very nice. I'm relying on you to keep them all out of mischief."

Mumbling something about getting more potatoes, Jennie hurried out of the room. Her mother, noticing her mood, motioned to Eric to find out what was troubling her.

Eric found her in the kitchen, her face flushed and angry.

"What's the matter, Jennie?" he asked quietly. "Or is it none of my business?"

"Oh, it's your business all right," she said quickly.

30

"Like the folk in those American pictures—you play quite a star role."

"Because I ran in that race yesterday?"

"I'm not blaming you, Eric. Sandy blackmailed you into it. You had no choice but to run. I asked him, pleaded with him, to leave you alone."

Eric gently put his hands on her shoulders and looked into her eyes. "Listen, Jen, Sandy's the university Captain, athletics are his life, and I know how much he enjoyed the race. Running's harmless enough. You can't blame Sandy for trying to get me into it. Anyway, I enjoyed the race."

"Athletics may be Sandy's life, but what's your life, Eric? That's what concerns me."

"Away with you, Jennie. It's just a bit of fun, that's all."

"It's not fun, Eric, and it's not in you to regard it as such. But be honest with me. How much time will you have left for God?"

There was no easy answer. Eric's father, who understood Jennie's attitude, tried to help his son when they were sitting later by the fireside.

"You're a very lucky young man, Eric," said his father. "You're the proud possessor of many gifts and it's your sacred duty to put them to good use. You know, I'm fast coming to the belief that God's a Scot. He's benevolent, sure, but shrewd with it. He'd not want you to waste all that speed just catching the bus in the morning."

"But Jennie's right about time," Eric said, trying to be fair to his sister. "It's going to take time. Something's got to suffer."

"How good are you as a runner, Eric?"

"Yesterday in that race," Eric replied slowly, "I had a glimpse, a feeling, I've never had before—of almost unlimited power. Sandy reckons I can run for Scotland before the month's out, and after that the sky's the limit."

"Meaning what?" asked his father.

"The Olympic Games, maybe."

"Eric," said his father, "you can praise the Lord by peeling a potato if you peel it to perfection. Run in His name . . . and let the world stand back in wonder."

"And what about Jennie?"

"Don't you worry about Jennie. Just wait until she sees your name in the headlines."

Eric smiled wistfully. He wished Jennie could be won over so easily. But he knew how obstinate his sister was. And perhaps she was right after all, he thought.

But Eric followed his father's advice. He began to run regularly, training seriously with Sandy McGrath as his unofficial coach. He went up into the hills every day, developing his stamina as much as his speed. Loping across a hillside in his wild style, he might have been mistaken for a deer running for cover. His sense of the power within him grew with every race. His name already known from his rugby games, he was soon chosen to run for Scotland. His astonishing speed and his strange style were talked about by runners across the border in England. He was called The Flying Scot. It wasn't long before Harold

Abrahams at Cambridge heard of his successes and fast times. The Flying Scot was a future rival, Harold decided.

As the months flashed by and the year 1922 came to an end and 1923 began, Eric struggled to give equal time to his missionary work, trying to satisfy Jennie. Wherever he ran, he always preached a sermon and frequently used running as an example of how to live.

After the Athletics International between Scotland and Ireland in Edinburgh on May 16, 1923, Eric addressed a crowd in heavy rain. Standing under an umbrella on a small platform, Eric said, "You came to see a race today, see someone win. It happened to be me." There was laughter under all the other umbrellas. "But I want you to do more than just watch a race. I want you to take part in it. I want to compare faith to running in a race. It's hard, requires concentration of will, energy of soul. You experience elation when the winner breaks the tape, especially if you've got a bet on it." More laughter. "But how long does that last? You go home maybe to your dinner and it's burnt. Maybe you haven't got a job. . . . So who am I to say 'believe,' 'have faith' in the face of life's realities. I would like to give you something more permanent, but I can only point the way. I have no formula for winning the race. Everyone runs in his or her own way. Then where does the power come from to see the race to its end?"

With the rain running down his face, Eric moved closer to the crowd. "The power comes from within," he said. "Jesus told us, 'Behold, the Kingdom of God is within you. If with all your hearts, you truly seek me, you shall ever surely find me.' If you commit yourself to the love of Christ, then that is how you run the straight race.''

Eric stepped off the platform, waving to his rain-soaked congregation. ''Cheers! Thank you all for coming.''

At the same time, Harold Abrahams was competing in international athletics meetings. He was on the English team that faced tough Dutch competition in track and field events. He did well in the long jump and the hurdles, but his main interest was still in the 100 meters sprint. He intended to prove at the next Olympic Games that he was the fastest man on earth.

His fame had already spread far beyond Cambridge and gave him a special place in the university's life. He was no longer Abrahams the Jew, but Abrahams the runner. Children stopped him in the Cambridge streets for his autograph, which gave him great satisfaction. But the Olympic Games to be held in Paris next year were seldom far from his mind. The Flying Scot, Eric Liddell, was his main rival among British runners. He wanted to beat Liddell before the British team was selected for the Olympics.

When Eric ran for Scotland against France in another international athletics meeting, Harold travelled up to Edinburgh to watch him. Surely Liddell had some weaknesses. He had been told that the Scot's technique was faulty, but his track tactics were usually very sound. After all, Liddell, like Abrahams, had yet to lose.

Harold watched the runners line up for the 440 yards race. He recognized Eric Liddell immediately from his newspaper pictures. Harold was amazed at the young Scottish runner's relaxed, untroubled manner as he waited for the start. Eric even wished his French opponents good luck in their own language. He seemed to lack the competitive drive that Harold associated with great running and yet his record spoke for itself. He was a winner. Well, he'll be a loser when we meet, Harold thought as he stared from the grandstand at the calm Liddell. Winning was more important to Harold than ever. He needed to win. He could no more have wished his opponents good luck like Liddell than he could have imagined losing.

The race that day was held on a converted rugby ground. Everything was rather primitive, including the scoreboards and the spectator stands. There were no separate lanes for the runners; the man who had the inside position had a big advantage. Harold wondered how Liddell would solve the problem since the Scot was starting on the outside.

The gun cracked and the runners were off to a fast start. A Frenchman took the lead, with Eric Liddell close behind him. Suddenly as Eric drew even, the French runner elbowed him off the track. Caught completely by surprise, Eric stumbled on the grass and fell over. A gasp went up from the great Scottish crowd at the collapse of their hero. Harold sat forward, horrified. He had wasted his time coming up to Edinburgh. Liddell wouldn't have a chance to show anything now. The race was over for him.

Yet Harold was wrong. For a few seconds that seemed an eternity to the watching crowd, Eric lay on his back. The other runners were already far down the track. But then, suddenly, as if a surge of new power had passed through him, Eric sprang to life again. In one quick leap, he was on his feet and was off down the track in pursuit of the others. The crowd applauded his courage, but he had lost so much ground he could never catch up. Yet that clearly wasn't Eric's view. He ran like a man inspired, his head thrown back, his feet pounding wildly, his arms whirling with the intensity of his effort. It still seemed hopeless and yet he began to gain on the other runners. They were still twenty yards in front. Then only nineteen, eighteen, seventeen. . . . Relentlessly Eric cut the distance separating him from the pack, until he reached those at the back and swept past them. By the time the home stretch was reached, Eric was running fourth, about ten yards behind the leader—the Frenchman who had elbowed him off the track.

The crowd roared encouragement. Harold sat on the edge of his seat, marvelling at Eric's superb running. It still seemed impossible that he could catch up ten more yards, but Eric's head thrust farther back, his arms rose higher, his legs flashed over the ground. Forty yards from the finish, he was third and seemed about to collapse, his mouth wide open gasping for air, but he refused to give up. Then, from somewhere within, he found a fresh burst of energy that carried him into second place. The crowd rose to its feet in excitement. He had a chance, a definite chance of winning.

Harold watched with astonishment as Eric swept into the lead and breasted the tape two yards ahead of the Frenchman—and then fell exhausted into the arms of officials. They half-carried him to the side of the track and laid him gently on the grass, his eyes closed, only half-conscious. He had spent everything he had and hardly heard the great roars of his fellow Scots.

A little man in a baggy suit with a straw hat at a rakish angle knelt down beside Eric. He was Sam Mussabini, half Italian, half Arab, and probably the best trainer of sprinters in Europe. Mussabini's new methods of training and his contempt for the lack of professionalism in sports had made him a controversial figure.

He told people now to get back, to give Eric air. He expertly kneaded Eric's stomach with the flat of his hand. Eric's labored breathing slowly became easier and his eyes half-opened.

"Mr. Liddell," said Sam gently, "that wasn't the prettiest quarter of a mile I've ever seen, but it was the bravest."

Eric grinned wearily. Sandy McGrath pushed through the crowd and leaned over him. He was relieved to see Eric was conscious. It had been a tremendous effort even for him.

"Well done, Eric, well done. You'll be all right in a jiffy."

"You take good care of this lad of yours, Mr. McGrath," Sam said, "because if you lose him, you'll never find another one like him. Get him up now."

Sam and Sandy together helped Eric to his feet.

"Come on, son," said Sam. "Keep your arm way out."

Sandy helped Eric through the cheering crowd. Sam applauded, too. He knew a truly great runner when he saw one.

"Mr. Mussabini," said a voice behind him.

It was Harold.

"Well, now," said Sam, mildly surprised, "Mr. Abrahams, isn't it? And what can I do for you?"

"I came up from Cambridge to see you — you and Eric Liddell. I'd heard you were *both* the best."

"And what d'you think now?" asked Sam with a sly smile.

"About Eric Liddell? I've never seen such drive, such commitment in a runner — he runs like a wild animal. He unnerves me."

"So he should. He'd scare the living daylights out of me."

"Yes," said Harold quietly, "and I want you to help me take him on."

Sam fumbled in his pocket for matches to light a cigar. He studied the forceful young man facing him.

"Are you married, Mr. Abrahams?"

"No, why?"

"Well, when the right girl comes along, how will you feel if she pops the question? You see, Mr. Abrahams, like the bridegroom, it's the coach that should do the asking."

"Mr. Mussabini," Harold said, his dark, intense eyes pleading with the little man, "I can run fast. With your help, I think I can even run faster, perhaps faster than any man ever ran. I want an Olympic gold medal to prove I'm the best." It was clear that all of Harold Abrahams' feelings were behind that remark. He had never talked so frankly to anyone except his friend Aubrey Montague. He knew he had to level with Sam Mussabini to have any chance of getting his help. "I can see an Olympic medal waiting for me . . . but I can't get it on my own."

Sam puffed on his cigar. "We've an old saying in my game. You can't put in what God's left out. Now you leave it to me, Mr. Abrahams. I'll watch you, I'll observe, and if I think I can help, if I can see the big prize hanging there, believe me I won't waste any time. When we meet again, I'll be the one that does the begging."

"So you will watch me?" Harold said quietly.

"Son, if you're good enough, I'll take you apart, piece by bloody piece."

"Thank you," said Harold, meaning it. He couldn't hope for more from the little man with the straw hat. He had to prove himself first. He would have to take on Eric Liddell without Sam's help. He remembered the Scot's extraordinary recovery, that unbelievable mad dash that made up twenty yards. The man must have the heart of a lion. He did everything wrong and yet it made no difference. The sheer power and drive in that Scot's body were greater than he had ever seen in a runner. It would take a lot to beat him.

Harold's eyes flashed with pride. He had never been beaten by anyone. He hadn't come this far to lose to Eric Liddell. The sooner they raced and settled who was the faster, the better.

Only One Gets the Prize

> Do you not know that in a race all the runners run, but only
> one gets the prize? Run in such a way as to get the prize. Ev-
> eryone who competes in the games goes into strict training.
> They do it to get a crown that will not last; but we do it to get
> a crown that will last forever. Therefore I do not run like a
> man running aimlessly; I do not fight like a man beating the
> air. No, I beat my body and make it my slave so that after I
> have preached to others, I myself will not be disqualified for
> the prize.
>
> *1 Corinthians 9:24–27, NIV*

As we are introduced to Eric Liddell, we are immediately drawn to his gentleness, to a man calmly at
peace with himself and God. The opening scene,
where Eric is found graciously signing autographs and
encouraging the children in their athletic endeavors,
suggests a man willing to serve others. As we get to

know him, we find a man who has determined his priorities but is not without the wisdom to change course, should he feel God's gentle nudge.

Eric was an established rugby star drawn to running under the guidance of his friend, Sandy McGrath. It was subtle at first, starting with a friendly outing, but gradually requiring more planning and training. Eric had been raised in a Christian missionary family, and had been taught the Biblical principle of authority, seeking his father's wisdom and advice. One has to wonder what turn of events there might have been had his father rejected Eric's desire to excel in running. Instead, though, his father challenges Eric to give God the very best of his talent for running. Eric responds with greater intensity in his training. His notoriety as a runner grows while he continues to acknowledge God as the most important influence in his life.

Eric manages to be selfless and Christian, while not alienating himself from the world's ways. His encounter with the young Scottish boy after church one Sunday is illustrative. Eric intercepts the young boy's ball as he and his sister, Jennie, leave church. He gently admonishes the boy about keeping God's day holy, yet offers to play him and his whole family early the next morning before he departs. He presents a picture of a friendly God, a loving God, not a spoilsport kind of God.

I see in Eric an easiness as he walks with Jesus and allows himself to be yielded to God's will. In stark contrast is Jennie, whose relationship with the Lord is extremely intense. She is absolutely blinded to the possibility of letting Jesus live through Eric's running. How can God possibly be glorified in any other realm besides the missionary field? We empathize with her desire to protect Eric from compromising his relationship with Jesus. However, we find ourselves defending Eric from her, realizing that our Lord can be glorified in all areas of life, as long as Jesus is always pre-eminent in our motives and actions.

God is never limited to a stone building, an organization, or one man's way of executing a plan. His love knows no limits. We all know God is love, but we need to understand that His love can manifest itself through our family interactions, business dealings, athletic abilities, and in the clasroom. Eric Liddell is a superb example of this type of relationship to God. With his rare gift for running — inspired though technically flawed — Eric celebrates the glory of the Lord, and God is manifested through him.

We have a superb example in this chapter of how we can either be overcome by life's adversities or we can choose to overcome them. In his race in France, Eric is purposely knocked off the track by an opponent. In a moment, he instinctively chooses to fight the battle, to continue the race. Instead of giving up, he gives it his all and is victorious in the true sense of the word.

Questions for Reflection and Discussion

1. Jesus said that no man can serve two masters, God and mammon, because he will love one and hate the other. Eric Liddell was a servant to mankind, choosing to preach the gospel as well as to worship God. Whom do you serve? Whom do you worship? And why?

2. Eric's sister, Jennie, recognized the potential spiritual danger Eric faced. He was a student, he was preaching the good news, and now he was taking on the rigors of training to run. She was concerned that he was trying to accomplish too much and would lose his relationship with his first love, Jesus Christ. Do you feel at times that your life strains you to unbearable limits? If so, what could you trim from your activities that would make you better able to know and serve and be used by God's Holy Spirit?

3. Eric Liddell takes the opportunity afforded him as a renowned athlete to share the insight that Jesus was the very giver of his talent and his life. He was not an ordained minister of the church, but lived out the word of God everywhere, at any time. Do you have to be an Eric Liddell in order to show how Jesus continually works through your life? Are you using every opportunity given to you to preach the good news, whether it be on the job, on the street, in the restaurant, or to the salesman who comes to your door? How do you do this?

4. Harold Abrahams expressed his feelings behind his motives for an Olympic gold medal when he said, "I want an Olympic gold medal to prove I'm the best." Do you evaluate your walk with Christ based on worldly guidelines? Do you have to be materially prosperous to receive God's grace? Do we have to win Olympic gold medals to prove that we are the best?

5. Eric's running technique was unorthodox; but while he did everything wrong, it made no difference. Eric's style was not a trained one, yet God's gifts were manifest in him. Eric gave God his best, and

God did the rest. Do you allow your inadequacies to steal from your ministry to others? What great lengths can you attain for God's glory if you simply place your faith and your will in the will of God?

6. In James, it says for us to count it all joy when we experience triumph. In Eric's 440-yard race, in France, he is elbowed to the ground. He responds by getting onto his feet and chasing after the other runners. He accepts the challenge. When problems come your way, do you admit defeat, or do you see them as an opportunity to grow closer to God, to grow stronger in His character. Do you count it all joy?

4

Aubrey Montague was worried. His friend Harold was neglecting everything except his running. He no longer seemed to care about his university studies or his other college activities. All that mattered was conditioning his body to produce the maximum speed to beat Eric Liddell.

Watching Harold practicing an even faster start, Aubrey suspected that the Scottish runner now represented all that Harold felt he was competing against in the world. The fair-haired, modest Liddell, so secure in his Christian beliefs and so spontaneous in his running, was certainly the opposite of Harold, the dark, defensive competitor, driven by a need to prove himself continually. Beating Liddell would be the same to Harold as beating the world that tried to shut him out. It was unfair to Liddell, but Harold needed to relate his running to his deepest personal feelings in order to achieve his incredible drive.

Certainly beating Eric Liddell had become an obsession with Harold. It wasn't a healthy state of mind, Aubrey decided, so when he and several other students, including Andy, decided to spend a wild weekend in London, he pressed Harold to join them. A weekend off was just what he needed. At first Harold wasn't interested, he couldn't spare the time, but Aubrey argued that all work and no play were making him far too tense as a runner and a short break would help both his muscles and his mental attitude. Much to Aubrey's surprise, Harold finally agreed. And being Harold, he soon took over and dominated their London trip.

The high point for everyone was visiting the Savoy Theatre, where the original D'Oyly Carte productions of Gilbert and Sullivan operettas were presented. They watched a performance of *The Mikado* from a special box just above the stage. They were dressed in formal evening attire, black ties and tails with bow ties. As each of them in turn peered through opera-glasses, they all fell in love with the same actress—a very pretty young soprano. But none of them did anything about it, except Harold. He left them in the theater bar between acts, saying he would be back shortly.

Andy winked. "So the man with the stone heart's frail after all. Abrahams is smitten."

"Smitten?" said Aubrey. "He's decapitated. He won't listen to reason. He's gone to talk to her."

"Good for him," cried Andy, buying them all a glass of champagne. "Here, hold Harold's glass for him. He may need it."

Harold soon appeared beside them. He raised the glass extended to him by Aubrey.

"Cheers!"

The others watched him curiously, but Harold gave nothing away. At last Andy couldn't wait any longer.

"Well?"

"Well what?" demanded Harold.

"Did you speak to her?"

"Yes," he said with a pleased expression.

"What did she say?"

"She accepted my invitation to dinner."

"To dinner!"

Andy was obviously unsure whether to believe him. So were the others. Harold felt he had to explain.

"She knew my name already. She has a kid brother who's mad for athletics. He never stops talking about me, she said."

The others raised their champagne glasses to him. Harold acknowledged their tribute with a gleeful smile. He looked as pleased as if he had won a race. Clearly Harold had to bring his strong competitive urge even into his personal life, thought Aubrey.

The pretty young soprano, dark and slender with bright teasing eyes, was named Sybil Gordon. She introduced Harold to her favorite restaurant near the Savoy Theatre, where the head waiter knew her and quickly found them a quiet table away from the crowd. When they had studied the menu and ordered, Sybil stared across the table at the tall young athlete, brimming with vitality and self-confidence.

"You don't look very ruthless," she said.

"Should I?"

"According to my brother, that's why you always win." She sat back and assessed her handsome escort. "Why running?"

"Why singing?" asked Harold in the same amused tone.

"It's my job. . . . No, that's silly. I do it because I love it. Do you love running?"

"I'm more of an addict. It's a compulsion, a weapon."

"Against what?"

"Being Jewish, I suppose."

Sybil laughed. "You're not serious?"

"You're not Jewish or you wouldn't ask."

"Fiddlesticks! People don't care. Anyway, being Jewish hasn't done you any harm."

"I'm what I call semi-deprived," replied Harold.

"That sounds clever. What does it mean?"

"It means they lead me to water but they won't let me drink."

Sybil leaned across the table to look into his eyes. "You're a funny old stick, Mr. Harold Abrahams. Funny, but fascinating."

She put her hand over his on the table. "Life isn't that gloomy, is it?"

"Not tonight. You're so beautiful."

She squeezed his hand. "Thank you."

He deliberately set out to charm her. He gently caressed her hand. His dark eyes stared into hers. The noisy, elegant surroundings were all but forgotten. Even their food and drinks remained untouched. As he felt her re-

48

sponding to him, his self-confidence grew. If he could win this beautiful young singer desired by so many men, then nothing surely was beyond him, not even beating Eric Liddell.

The race of the century, as many in the British Isles called it, was arranged at last.

Eric, "The Flying Scot," travelled to London for the race on the famous express train, *The Flying Scotsman*, and newspapers made much of the coincidence.

He was treated like a celebrity on the express.

An attendant, who woke him in his sleeping compartment as the train arrived at King's Cross Station in the center of London, showed him the morning newspapers with his picture prominently displayed.

"Expecting great things from all accounts," the attendant said jovially.

"Are they, indeed?" said Eric, rubbing the sleep from his eyes.

So much fuss about a race amused him. What would Jennie say?

"Take your time, sir. You've still got an hour," said the attendant as he went out. "Good luck this afternoon."

"Thank you." Eric spread one of the newspapers open at the sports page.

He read: "FLYING SCOT COMES SOUTH TO TACKLE CREAM OF CAMBRIDGE. ABRAHAMS SAYS 'I'M READY.'"

Aye, Mr. Abrahams, thought Eric. *So's the Scot*.

The race was part of the British Games and the outstanding athletes were sure of a place on the Olympic team.

The huge communal dressing room was tense with a feeling of competition, of so many rivals within touching distance. But the most famous competitors, Harold Abrahams and Eric Liddell, were placed on opposite sides of the huge room. Nobody spoke to them. A slightly eerie, subdued atmosphere reflected the feelings of the runners. They spoke in hushed, reverent tones, not wishing to jangle tightly drawn nerves.

Harold was totally withdrawn. He might have been alone. He stood carefully unpacking his meticulously arranged attaché case. His nerves screamed with mounting tension, but outwardly he was as calm as a surgeon taking out his instruments for a routine operation. First, he laid out his running vest, shorts, and towel. Then his spiked shoes, highly polished, a cork on each spike. Then his shining trowel for digging his starting holes. Then his cricket style sweater and college blazer. And finally his rubbing oils for his body.

Aubrey watched him, wanting to speak, but not daring to. Harold's concentration before a race was complete; any interruptions, even from a close friend like Aubrey, made him angry. He was even more detached before this race—the last big test before the Olympic trials.

On the far side of the room, Eric pulled on his Edinburgh University vest, as calm as ever, not even glancing in Harold's direction. He turned up the collar of his blazer in the accepted style and quickly combed his hair. Then he deliberately stared across at Harold and slowly crossed the room toward him.

All the hushed conversations ceased. Everybody waited for the confrontation between the two great rivals. As Eric approached, Harold bent over his attaché case, apparently unaware of what was happening.

"Mr. Abrahams?"

Harold glanced up casually.

"Mr. Liddell."

The two great runners eyed each other respectfully.

"I'd like to wish you the best of success," Eric said.

"Thank you," Harold replied, shaking hands, "and may the best man win."

Somewhere in the excited crowd of thousands was Sybil Gordon, but Harold shut out all thoughts of her. No one existed for the next few minutes but Abrahams (Number 30) and Liddell (Number 14). Today he had to make his supreme effort and run faster than he had ever run before.

He was hardly aware of the lineup or of digging the starting hole. Unblinkingly, he kept his eyes fixed on Liddell, as if trying to read the Scot's thoughts. The 100-meter race would be won on temperament as much as conditioning, because they were both superbly fit. If either of them failed in their physical drive or showed a moment's hesitation, the other would win. This was the race he had been waiting for, training for, torturing himself for, all these weeks. He would run Eric Liddell into the ground. He had to.

Liddell was so damned calm, Harold thought. If he hadn't seen the man run, he would have dismissed him as too matter-of-fact. A runner needed a little tension to be at his best, to be as alert as if balanced on a knife edge, or that was what he had always believed until he observed Liddell. The Scot had the same relaxed, sporting composure as Andy — they were both of the Christian Establishment in their way. He, Harold Abrahams, was the outsider. Well, the outsider would win today.

"Get to your marks."

A hushed crowd sat forward in the stadium.

"Get set."

The starter's pistol rose. Harold felt all his nerves strain, ready for action. He tried to forget Liddell and the other four runners and simply concentrate.

The pistol went off.

Harold shot forward like an arrow. But so did Liddell. They raced neck-and-neck, then Eric took the lead, Harold at his shoulder.

Harold summoned all his reserves for an extra thrust to carry him past Eric. It always worked. It always took him ahead. Nobody could match it.

But as Harold drove himself to his fastest pace, Eric's head went back, his arms whirled. He was a foot ahead, flat out. Harold's great drive had been matched.

Desperate, with a strange feeling of unreality, Harold glanced across at Liddell and at that moment he lost any chance of winning. He had broken his concentration and checked his momentum.

Eric, his mind, body and spirit working as one, ignoring his opponents, swept ahead with complete confidence and breasted the tape like a man possessed.

Harold was just behind — a step behind, but it might have been a mile.

His face was full of pain and disbelief.

He had *lost*.

It was a nightmare come true.

Liddell was the winner, not he.

Liddell had beaten him.

He had *lost, lost, lost!*

He couldn't accept it.

I've never lost, he'd once told Aubrey.

He'd always believed he never would.

Well, now he had.

The impossible had happened.

For more than an hour afterwards, he sat in the empty stadium re-running the race in his mind as if he could change the result. Over and over again, he replayed the finish. But the result was the same.

If only he hadn't glanced across at Liddell!

He had doubted himself.

Sybil found him staring fixedly at the track. She

watched him uneasily. This was a new Harold she had never seen before—a Harold with no self-confidence, a beaten Harold. Her beautiful face frowned with concern. She had to try to help him, to bring him back from his nightmare of defeat. He was too vulnerable under his aggressive manner; his ego was badly wounded. What had he said about his running? It was "a weapon." Well, the weapon had not been enough today. Sympathy would do no good. She had to arouse his competitive spirit if she could.

"Harold! Harold!" she cried as she approached. "This is absolutely ridiculous. It's a race you've lost, not a relative. Nobody's dead."

Harold didn't reply; he might not have heard her. His silence annoyed her; she wasn't used to being ignored. She felt shut out.

"For goodness sake, snap out of it, Harold. You're behaving like a child."

"I lost," he groaned.

"I know. I was there, remember, watching?" She put her hand on his arm, wanting to touch him. "It was marvellous. You were marvellous. He was more marvellous, that's all." She withdrew her hand as he hadn't responded; she mustn't treat him like a child. "On this day, the best man won."

That stirred Harold. He said slowly, almost as if speaking to himself, "I had to look for him. It's absolutely fundamental—you never look."

"He was ahead. There was nothing you could have done. He won fair and square."

"I'm finished. My running's over."

54

"Well, if you can't take a beating, perhaps it's for the best."

Harold said impatiently, "I don't run to take beatings. I run to win. If I can't win, I won't run."

"If you don't run, you can't win," said Sybil sharply. She was suddenly angry with him. "Phone me when you've worked that one out." She began to walk away.

Harold cried, "Sybil, don't go. I just don't know what to do."

"Try growing up."

"Please . . ."

His desperate tone touched her. She came back to him.

She said gently, "Harold, you're a great man. You ran like a god. I was proud of you. Don't make me ashamed."

"It's not the losing, Syb." He closed his eyes, trying to explain. "Eric Liddell's a fine man and a fine runner. It's me. After all that work, I lost, and now God knows what do I aim for?"

"Beating him the next time."

The race flashed through Harold's head again, Liddell matching his finest effort and thrusting ahead.

"Sybil, I can't run any faster."

It was a cry from the depths of his despair.

"I beg to differ, Mr. Abrahams," a voice interrupted. "I can find you another two yards."

Standing below them at the edge of the stands, smiling and chewing on a cigar, was Sam Mussabini. He touched his straw hat in tribute to Sybil.

Harold sat up, slowly grasping the meaning of what Sam had said.

The great trainer was willing to work with him even though he'd lost.

Another two yards—that would have been enough to beat Liddell.

There was hope for him yet.

Let Not Your Hearts Be Troubled

> Peace I leave with you; my peace I give to you. . . . Let not your hearts be troubled, neither let them be afraid.
>
> *John 14:27, RSV*

Have you ever felt the compulsion to win at everything you do? One of our characters, Harold Abrahams, has that innate compulsion to excel and to win at all costs. His singleness of purpose in excelling at his running is of increasing concern to his friend, Aubrey Montague. When Aubrey suggests a weekend theater diversion in London, it takes much perseverance on Aubrey's part to convince Harold that all work and no play could be detrimental to his training. Aubrey's persuasion brings a slight turn of events in Harold's life when Harold is smitten with the lead soprano in *The Mikado*. We get a glimpse of Harold's workaholic character in his need to win even the heart of the young Sybil Gordon. He wastes no time in inviting her for dinner, the start to winning her heart. Our thoughts move with those of Aubrey's: "Clearly Harold had to bring his strong competitive urge even into his personal life." This for Harold is a way of life. He has known no other, so he considers each opportunity one to be conquered.

As Harold senses Sybil's response to him, he thinks that "if he could win this beautiful young singer, desired by so many men, then nothing surely was beyond him, not even beating Eric Liddell." However, this picture of supreme confidence collapses a little later during "the race of the century," held in London as partial selection for the British Olympic team. Following the usual pre-race preparations, which include Eric Liddell's greeting of encouragement to Harold, we find ourselves on the starting line. A startling break in Harold's self-confidence becomes apparent as we note his attention centered more on Eric than his own race. Curiosity consumes Harold as if he would give anything to know Eric's secret of success. Harold questions his own abilities at a time when self-confidence is of the utmost importance. After the race starts and just before the finish, Harold breaks his concentration to check Eric's position—an enormous strategical mistake. Rather than running his own race, Harold is far too concerned about his competition. He doubts himself.

Defeated by Liddell, Harold cannot cope with his new status as runner-up. He is perilously near an identity crisis when in walks Harold's salvation, trainer Sam Mussabini. Mr. Mussabini promises to help him gain another two yards, offering Harold hope for beating Eric and becoming the fastest human in the world.

Questions for Reflection and Discussion

1. The desire to win at all costs and the desire to excel at whatever you do often become confused. The first is selfish; the second develops character. Are there areas in your life where you need to evaluate your desires?
2. Harold's new relationship with Sybil allows us to see him in a more vulnerable position. He begins to respond to her challenge to "grow up." Are there people in your life who call you to maturity? How does God call you to maturity in Christ?
3. Harold is very aware of Eric's calm before and during the race. In fact, that awareness—to the detriment of his own concentration—contributes to Harold's defeat. The temptation to worry about the competition is strong. What can you do to eliminate this worry?
4. Defeat is something most of us experience on a regular basis, but losing a race came as a shock to Harold. How do you cope with defeat?

5

Sam Mussabini started work on Harold at once. He subtly restored Harold's self-confidence by showing him lantern slides of other great sprinters.

Harold carefully studied the faces of his rivals projected onto the wall of his room at Caius College. Sam identified each man.

"Charlie Paddock, the California Cannonball . . . world's fastest human. Winner of the 100 meters at the Olympic Games in Antwerp in 1920. Time—10.3 seconds."

Sam pointed to another face. "Jackson Scholtz, the New York Thunderbolt . . . runner-up in the Olympic Games of 1920. Lost by looking right." He put in another slide. "Here it is—the finish. You see Paddock leaping past him at the tape. That glance cost Scholtz the race. Scholtz is the fastest."

"Ten point three—four," Harold corrected himself.

Sam put in another slide with a sly grin. A familiar face filled the wall. "Eric Liddell—well, you know all about him." He stared solemnly at Harold. "Look at them. Think them. Breathe them. I want their faces leering at you every time you shut your eyes."

"The Flying Scot first," said Harold. "That bloody well hurt."

"Eric Liddell? He's no real problem. Oh, he's a great runner, but he needs to go further out. Longer, the quarter, he's no hundred meters man."

"He could've fooled me."

"Oh, he's fast all right," said Sam. "But he won't go any faster, not in the dash anyway. He's a gut runner—all heart. He digs deep. But a short sprint's run on nerves. It's tailor-made for neurotics."

"Thanks very much."

"I mean it, Harold. You need to push guts, bully 'em, put 'em under strain, to get at your best. In ten seconds, there's no time for that. You have to hone nerves for a sprint, sharpen 'em up, give 'em a precision."

"So I'm an unhoned neurotic."

Sam grinned. "I couldn't have put it better myself." He puffed on his cigar while Harold examined the three faces.

"Paddock, Scholtz, Liddell."

Sam placed a long line of pennies on a table.

"Come over here, Mr. Abrahams. Fifty coins—each one a stride in your hundred yards. I know, I counted them."

"That many?"

"Aye, and not enough. Do you know why you lost the other day? Because you're overstriding—just a couple of inches."

"But I've always run like that—it's natural."

"Natural or not," grunted Sam, "it's death to a sprinter. It's like a slap in the face each stride you take." He slapped Harold sharply on the cheek. "Knocks you back like that."

Sam slapped Harold again. "And that!" Harold winced, but didn't move. "And that!" Sam laughed. "Now let's see the slides of you running." Harold in mid-stride was projected on to the wall. "Ha! There! D'you see that? There's your center of gravity. You've got to keep beneath it to retain your impetus. Look at your leading foot—two inches too far—and there's your slap in the face. You're overstriding, Mr. Abrahams."

"What can we do about it?"

Sam strode over to the metronome on the top of Harold's piano. Sam started it moving.

"Tick-tock! Tick-tock! Tick-tock!"

"Look," Sam said, "this gadget here represents your running rhythm—'Tick-tock, tick-tock.' It's what we call 'cadence.' Now what we'll do with you is . . . this!" And he adjusted the metronome to a slightly faster rhythm. He clapped his hands. "That's you, Mr. Abrahams—the new stride we shall develop."

The weeks that followed were grueling ones for Harold. Sam Mussabini cleverly recruited Sybil to be his assistant. Her presence helped to lighten the strain of starting a new round of exhausting training sessions so soon after his long preparations for Liddell. Sam had evolved his own methods and his exercises were strenuous. Harold found himself running stiff-legged, flexing his ankles like a prancing horse.

"Now I want you to imagine you're running on hot bricks," Sam told him. "If you leave your feet too long on the ground, they'll get burnt, right? Up, up, up. Light as a feather, Mr. Abrahams."

Sam ordered him about like a ringmaster from an open touring car, slowly changing Harold's stride and conditioning his body. Sybil held the stop watch when he ran.

"Don't react, Mr. Abrahams," Sam said at the beginning of a practice run. "Go for release—a coiled spring, a dam about to burst."

Sam marked the width of Harold's old stride across a sheet of paper, then measured the change—he was now two inches under.

"We're getting there, Mr. Abrahams."

For the next few weeks, Harold ran in all kinds of weather. It was common to see him appearing through the early morning mist. Harold, with his shorter stride, his cadence quicker, had never been so fast. Sam, elated, threw his straw hat in the air.

But there were grumbles at Cambridge about Harold and his professional coach; it went against the university's tradition in sport. "The Jew and the Wog," as Harold and Sam were called by many, were breaking the unwritten rules of the gentlemanly amateur.

Eric Liddell hadn't let his victory over Harold Abrahams relax him. His eyes were now on making the British team for the Olympics. He ran every day, urged on by Sandy McGrath and in spite of his sister Jennie's reproachful looks. He worked not so much on speed as stamina, but his training methods were crude compared with Sam Mussabini's. He still ran in the hills of the Highlands and on the beach, and it was always easy to tell when he was making his maximum effort because his head went far back on his shoulders.

But inevitably Eric's training sometimes made him late for his missionary work. Jennie finally erupted one afternoon when he came running into the mission hall halfway through a service. He tried to apologize, but she wouldn't listen.

"Training, training, training, all I ever hear is training, Eric," Jennie snapped. "Do you believe in what we're doing here or not?"

Eric picked up a pile of hymn books. "Look, Jennie, I'm sorry. I was late. I apologize."

"That's all very well, Eric," she said angrily.

"Look, I said I was sorry."

"To me? It's not me you've insulted."

"Oh, away with your bother. The Lord will not feel slighted at the missing of a bus."

At the end of the service, Jennie told him, "Your mind's not with us any more, Eric. It's full of running and starting and medals and pace. Your head's so full of running you've no room for standing still."

"Jennie, Jennie, don't fret yourself," Eric said gently.

"I do fret myself. I'm frightened for you. I'm frightened for what it all might do to you."

A young schoolgirl approached Eric to ask for his autograph.

"Do you want to pick yourself a pen?" Eric asked humorously, crouching over so the schoolgirl could select a pen from his jacket pocket. He quickly signed his name in the girl's autograph book. "There you are."

The girl gave him a look of open hero-worship. "Thanks, Mr. Liddell."

Eric went back to Jennie. "Come on, let's go for a walk. I've got something to say."

They walked out of Edinburgh far enough up a hillside to overlook the ancient city. The grey rooftops appeared like stepping stones leading to the great castle jutting out against the skyline.

"It's a sight and a half, isn't it, Jennie?" said Eric, staring back. "I'll be sad to leave it." He moved closer to her. "I've decided. I'm going back to China. The missionary service has accepted me."

Jennie hugged him. "Oh, Eric, I'm so pleased."

Eric said quietly, "But I've got a lot of running to do first." Her look of happiness vanished. "Jennie, Jennie, you've got to understand. I believe that God made me for a purpose. For China. But He also made me fast, and when I run I feel His pleasure. To give it up would be to hold Him in contempt. You were right—it's not just fun. To win is to honor Him. Jennie, I've got my degree to get—all that work and then there's the Olympics in Paris. There's just not enough of me. I'm asking you to manage the Mission on your own until then. Will you do that for me, Jennie?"

Jennie didn't reply, but impulsively kissed his cheek. Eric smiled with relief.

While Harold was completing his training with Sam Mussabini, he received an invitation to dinner with the Master of Caius and his friend, the Master of Trinity. Harold suspected there was a reason for the invitation, that it wasn't to be just a social evening.

It was a very formal dinner, with elaborate wine-tastings that tested Harold's patience. He tried to be polite, waiting for the two old dons to get to the business of the dinner.

"Laid this wine down in 1914, the day war was declared," said the Master of Caius, "in a spirit of complete optimism and faith."

"It was the prevailing spirit," added the Master of Trinity.

"Cambridge was so sure, so buoyant, so confident then."

"A vanished world."

Both old men nodded in solemn agreement.

Harold tried to look politely interested. He envied the two old men their unassailable security, but he disliked their self-satisfied wallowing in the past and their intolerant conservatism. They were the enemy—the Establishment that kept him outside the gates.

"But yours is a fine generation, Abrahams," said the Master of Caius. "Marvellous in its promise. Those of you who survived or succeeded, you've helped us to have faith again in our task.''

"In the future, Abrahams.''

"I'm afraid we're the runt of the litter,'' Harold said.

"Never believe it,'' said the Master of Trinity. "We know. We know them, the lost generation. We know you. They will rest content.''

"They will, indeed, Abrahams,'' added the Master of Caius.

"Life slips by,'' said the Master of Trinity. "But this great country of ours, this fine old university, they offer some rare consolations, wouldn't you say?''

"Beyond measure, sir,'' said Harold.

"We can take it therefore,'' said the Master of Trinity, "you'd be acutely grieved to discover that some action or behavior on your part was causing this university grief?''

"Naturally, sir,'' replied Harold warily.

"Good! I was sure of it.''

The Master of Caius filled the wine glasses again.

Harold waited.

"We at Cambridge have long been proud of our athletic prowess,'' said the Master of Trinity. "We believe, have always believed, that our games are indispensable. They help mold the complete Englishman. They create character, foster courage, honesty and leadership. But most of all they imbue him with an unassailable spirit of loyalty, comradeship and mutual responsibility. Would you agree?''

"Yes, sir, I would,'' said Harold carefully.

"Abrahams, I'm afraid there is a growing suspicion in the bosom of this university—and I tell you this without in any way decrying your achievements in which we all rejoice—that, in your enthusiasm to succeed, you have perhaps lost sight of the latter."

The room was suddenly silent. The purpose of the dinner was now clear. The two dons regarded Harold coldly. He felt his anger rise, but struggled to suppress it.

"May I ask what form this disloyalty, this betrayal, takes?" he asked quietly.

"Oh! Hardly betrayal." The Master of Trinity touched his thin lips with a linen napkin.

"The word 'grief' *was* mentioned," said Harold.

"It's been said you have a personal coach," put in the Master of Caius accusingly.

"Mr. Mussabini, yes."

"Is he Italian?" inquired the Master of Trinity.

"Of Italian extraction."

"I see."

"But not all Italian."

"I'm relieved to hear it."

"He's half Arab."

"Do I take it that you employ this Mr. Mussabini on a professional basis?" asked the Master of Caius.

"Sam Mussabini is the finest, most advanced, clearest-thinking athletics coach in the country. I am honored that he considers me worthy of his complete attention."

"Nevertheless, he's a professional."

"What else would he be? He's the best."

"Well, there is where our paths diverge, Mr. Abrahams. The University believes that the way of the amateur can produce the most gratifying results."

"I am an amateur," Harold said.

"You are trained by a professional," snapped the Master of Trinity. "You have adopted a professional approach. For the past year you have concentrated wholly on developing your own technique, in the headlong pursuit, may I suggest, of individual glory. A policy hardly conducive to the fostering of 'esprit de corps.' "

Harold replied with rising anger, "I am a Cambridge man first and last. I am an Englishman first and last. What I have achieved, what I intend to achieve, is for my family, my university, and my country, and I bitterly resent your suggesting otherwise."

"Your aim, is it not," snapped the Master of Trinity, "is to win at all costs?"

"At all costs, no! But I do aim to win within the rules. Perhaps, sir, you would rather I played the gentleman . . . and lost."

"To playing the tradesman—yes!" said the Master of Trinity.

Harold's face flushed with anger.

"My boy," said the Master of Caius, "Your approach has been, shall we say, a little too artisan. You are the elite, and as such, must be seen to run rather to the manner born."

Harold put down his glass and stood up.

"Thank you for your hospitality," he told them. "The evening has been most illuminating."

He walked to the door, then his resentment overcame him, and he said sarcastically, "You know, gentlemen, you yearn for victory just as I do. But achieved with the apparent effortlessness of gods. Yours are the archaic values of the prep school playground. You deceive no one but yourselves. I believe in the relentless pursuit of excellence — and I'll carry the future with me!"

Harold Abrahams walked out, slamming the door behind him.

The two old dons looked at each other. Harold's actions had simply confirmed what they had felt all along.

"There departs a Semite," said the Master of Trinity. "A different God, a different mountain top."

Outside in the courtyard, Harold stood in the cold night air until his rage subsided. Those two bigots wouldn't have talked that way to Andy or Aubrey — or to Eric Liddell. He wasn't going to take it from them. They were just using Sam Mussabini as an excuse to get at him. He was still an outsider as far as they were concerned.

"Harold!"

Several dark figures approached him, led by Aubrey Montague, grinning broadly and waving a copy of the evening paper.

"The Olympic team's been chosen, Harold. You're in the 100 and 200, Andy has the 400 and hurdles, I have the steeplechase. . . ." He showed Harold the report in the paper. "Eric Liddell's picked, too — you'll be rivals under the same flag. Your chance to get even, what?"

To get even, yes, with them all, thought Harold.

"I can't wait," he told Aubrey.

He'd get his revenge on the biggest stage of all — the

Olympics. What would those two snobbish old dons say when he won a gold medal? He'd have the last laugh.

I Am Your God

> Fear not, for I am with you,
>   be not dismayed, for I am your God;
> I will strengthen you, I will help you,
>   I will uphold you with my victorious right hand.
>
> Isaiah 41:10, RSV

Everything seems to be working out for Harold Abrahams. He has secured Sam Mussabini as trainer and apparently won the heart of Sybil. Sam helps Harold gain the necessary two yards he promised by recognizing the need to change Harold's stride length. Countless hours are spent working on new technique and the psychological approach needed to win the gold medal. Sam admonishes Harold to eat, sleep, and breathe each of his prospective opponents. The attack is definitely not limited to just Eric Liddell any longer, but now includes the American champions, Jackson Scholtz and Charlie Paddock. "The Jew and the Wog" carefully avoid confrontation over the woman in Harold's life — the one person who could possibly distract Harold from his goal of the Olympics. Sam recruits Sybil as stop watch timer with one purpose in mind — to make the endeavor a united effort.

North of Cambridge, over the Scottish highlands and along the ocean beaches, Eric Liddell is making his own Olympic preparation in spite of his sister's reproachful attitude. Under the tutelage of Sandy McGrath, we note a marked difference in training compared to what is going on between Abrahams and Mussabini. While Harold and Sam concentrate on stride, quickness, and overall technique, Eric and Sandy emphasize stamina and endurance. Eric's focal point is so centered on his pursuit of excellence in training that it appears that all else has become secondary, including his missionary work, much to the distress of his sister, Jennie. As of yet, she has not caught the vision that Eric and his father share, that of running in God's name, to His glory. Eric is not alone in his personal testing.

Back at Cambridge, we find Harold openly accused of being too professional. The masters of Caius and Trinity have invited Harold to a formal dinner for just the three of them. Always on the defensive, Harold suspects that there is more to the invitation than merely wine tasting. His perception proves accurate, as these two old dons question Harold's interpretation of amateur athletics. At issue is the employment of a professional coach for personal gain. The fact that the coach happens to be half-Italian and half-Arab adds to their superior, elitist attitude that running is certainly beneath a Cambridge man's dignity.

A common thread throughout this chapter is that of fear. Fear is the motivating factor in Harold's headlong pursuit of the gold medal—fear that he could possibly lose again to Eric Liddell. Therefore, he employs the best in coaching expertise, Sam Mussabini. Sam, fearing that he may not command Harold's full attention and dedication, employs Sybil to help with the workout sessions. On the other hand, Jennie Liddell is frightened that Eric has filled his head with unimportant, nonessential racing details at the expense of his missionary work. She approaches her brother with her fear. Eric counters with a faith that is full of assurance that he is doing exactly what is pleasing to God. We see in Eric that there is no fear in doing what God has commanded; and in his serene, quiet manner, Eric explains to Jennie that there simply is not enough of him to go around. His priorities, given to him by the Lord, are to earn his degree, run in the Olympics to the glory of God, and then fulfill his call as a missionary.

Questions for Reflection and Discussion

1. What is the motivating force in your life? Are you controlled by fear or faith?
2. Proverbs 27:17 says that iron sharpens iron and one man sharpens another. Jennie was definitely an instrument of God to define Eric's priorities. Who is used, or who has been used, in your life to sharpen you into the likeness of Christ?

3. Eric's ability to keep calm under pressure is remarkable. When confronted by Jennie concerning his priorities, his quiet confidence reassures her. When under pressure, how do you react or respond to the situation at hand? Give an example.

4. Eric believed that his running was a positive expression of the will of the Lord. "When I run, I feel his pleasure." What area or areas of your life do you sincerely feel God finds pleasure in? What talents do you participate in where you feel God's delight and his joy?

5. In the process of pursuing excellence in his running ("You therefore must be perfect as your heavenly father is perfect," Matthew 5:48), Harold felt a need to eat, sleep, and breathe his training techniques. Is it a Christ-like attribute to pursue excellence to such a high degree? Can determination like Harold's — even in the pursuit of worldly gain — lead to the perfection demanded by the Lord, to become more and more like Him in our attitudes, our motivations, and our selflessness?

6

Just before the British Olympic team was to start its final weeks of training, Harold invited his parents to come to Cambridge. He offered no explanation. His busy father couldn't spare the time so his mother came alone, a small slender woman with intense black eyes and a mid-European face. Harold took her to hear the King's College Chapel choir. They sat in the narrow perpendicular chapel listening to the clear boyish voices rise upwards. Harold held himself proudly erect, his chin high. His mother's eye roamed over the historic Christian surroundings, wondering why Harold was so insistent that she spend time there. How had Cambridge affected her son? He was certainly more poised, more in control of his feelings—except where Sybil was concerned. He even allowed the young actress to interrupt his preparations for the Olympics.

"Why did you bring me here?" his mother whispered.

"You've always enjoyed singing," Harold whispered back. "There's none better."

"Is that the only reason?"

"What do you mean?"

"Now please, no nonsense, Harold. I'm your mother and I know you inside out. And if you ask me to sit in a Christian church and listen to Christian music, however beautiful, I want to know why."

Harold smiled. "Mother, I constantly underestimate you."

"You feel safer that way."

Afterwards, in a local tea-shop, his mother said, "Now tell me, does all this concern Sybil? You want to marry her?"

"I think so—yes! Would it hurt you if I did?"

"Harold, your father and I, we came to England with no illusions. We wanted freedom for ourselves and our children. But freedom means freedom. We love this country and want you to love it. Yet I'm a Jewish mother and I'd like you to love and marry a Jewish girl. But England, Cambridge—they are your reality. You want to belong to this world, and who am I to stand in your way?"

Harold gave his mother a quick, grateful look. "You understand me. But tell me this—why do I want to belong?" He glanced out at the busy Cambridge street. "This place . . . behind that charm out there, there's ugliness. I sensed it when I first arrived. I forget it, but then I'm reminded—brutally. And yet I still want to be part of it."

"And Sybil?" his mother asked quietly.

"Perhaps she's bound up in it, all this Englishness. Do I love her for herself or for what she represents? I've got to be sure. I don't want to hurt her."

"When do you go to Paris?"

"In two weeks. We go to Broadstairs to get ready first."

"Is Sybil going—to Paris, I mean?"

Harold shook his head. "No, she's singing."

"Good!"

"Why do you say that?"

"Harold, where is your problem of belonging? Your country has chosen you to be her champion against the world. How can you be more British? Sybil you can love for Sybil's sake—she brings you nothing you don't already have."

"It's not that simple, Mother. If I win, then maybe you're right. But the odds are against me. . . . Deep down I know that, and deep down I know that Sybil will be there still even if I lose."

"Harold, you're your father's son. You cross your bridges before they're even built. Tell the girl you must clear your mind of her for three weeks. You must give all your attention to the Olympics. It'll be hard, but I know her. She'll understand. Then go out there and *win*. When you come back, and you see her again, you'll know."

Harold brooded over her advice. It was easy to think that his mother was simply trying to break up his affair with Sybil. The two women had hit it off when they met, but his mother wanted a *Jewish* daughter-in-law, as she admitted. But she was usually fair and, where he was concerned, very shrewd. She knew all his moods, his strengths and his weaknesses. And it was true Sybil was taking time away from his training. His mind was on her

much of the time, affecting his concentration. His mother
was right. He *did* need to be alone for the last few weeks
before the great test—as alone and dedicated as a monk.

He felt his mother watching him anxiously. He looked
up and smiled at her.

"All right. I'll do it."

Sybil took it very hard, afraid Harold was dropping
her for good. His explanation didn't satisfy her. He had
let her take part in his training until now. What had
changed? Why couldn't she be around to keep him company at meals if she promised to leave him alone the rest
of the time? It wouldn't work, he said. He seemed
strangely nervous and unwilling to discuss his attitude
openly. What was he hiding from her?

She went to one of Harold's friends, Andy, to find out
if he knew anything.

Highbeck House was Andrew Lindsay's country home.
It was difficult to think of him as an Earl, but his home
was immense, a mansion in the middle of a vast green
estate.

He and Sybil strolled down a sloping lawn leading to a
lake, discussing Harold. Behind them came a butler carrying a silver tray of tea and a footman with a similar tray
of champagne. Sybil, looking beautiful in a light summer
coat and hat, sipped tea from a fine china cup, feeling
very grand. Andy, as elegantly casual as ever in an im-

maculate silk jacket, held a glass of champagne. Empty champagne glasses dotted the lawn and his makeshift running track beside the lake.

"He's darn difficult to love, old Harold," Andy said sympathetically. "He's in the minority, you see—makes 'em downright prejudiced . . . feel superior . . . can't relax . . . spend the whole damn time proving it . . . mostly to themselves."

Sybil listened impatiently. Andy was talking like a complacent Cambridge intellectual—or an Earl. Harold wasn't a social problem. Harold was Harold, the man she loved. But did she really know that passionate, aggressive man, who turned himself into a machine on the running track, the energy in him roaring up and driving him ahead of the other runners? She needed help, not a lecture. She interrupted Andy. "I've lost him. I can't reach him."

Andy sipped his champagne; his casualness irritated her when her world was tumbling down. "Don't worry, old girl. You'll reach him again, you will . . . after Paris. Now he can't help himself, poor chap. His great competitive drive has become like a demon and he's in the grip of it. Winning is more important than anything— even you. As a Jew, he feels the same way as the Welsh, the Scots, the Irish. 'Must win, can't do without it'— that kind of feeling. Who knows, perhaps it's because they can still only taste defeat."

Andy was lecturing again! She cut in. "He wants to 'clear his mind of me.' He can't *love* me and say that."

Andy motioned for more champagne and the butler quickly refilled his glass.

"Syb," he said firmly, "the world's against him—or so he believes. And now he has a chance to leave it wallowing in his wake. He can't see or hear anything beyond that . . . not even you. It's hard, but you've just got to try to understand."

"Why should I?"

"Because he's what you want—isn't he?"

"But why aren't you and Aubrey like that? Isn't the chance there for you, too?"

"To be *a* fastest, yes! But not *the* fastest. Faster than any man, ever before. That's immortality. Think what *that* means to a man like Harold. I don't need it. To me the whole thing's fun—to Harold, it's life and death."

What Andy said now made sense to her. Winning that gold medal had become a matter of life and death to Harold. She remembered how he had been immediately after losing to Eric Liddell. It was as if he had died for a short time.

"So all I can do is wait," she said.

"I'm afraid so, old girl. And hope like hell that he wins."

"And if he doesn't?"

"He'll start all over again. And he'll need your help to do it."

Sybil kissed him on the cheek.

"Thank you, Andy."

"A pleasure. Sure you can't stay for dinner?"

"I can't, Andy. I've got to be on stage at eight o'clock."

"Don't worry, Syb. I've never ever seen a man so taken as Harold is with you. He's a damn fool to risk losing you, but it's the price you have to pay for being in love with a great runner."

He sent Sybil to the Savoy Theatre in his chauffeur-driven Rolls-Royce and then went back to his own training. The butler had placed champagne glasses on a line of hurdles by the lake side, and he now filled each glass.

"Ready, your Lordship," the butler called to Andy.

"Now, men, if I shed a drop in going over, I want to know. Touch, but not spill, all right?"

Andy took off his silk jacket, revealing his running clothes and a right knee and shin scarred and bloody from training.

He crouched, concentrated, and exploded into a fast start. Skimming over each hurdle, his trailing right leg barely brushed the rough heavy wood. The champagne glasses shivered, but not a drop was spilled.

Andy nodded with satisfaction. This was his serious side other people rarely saw. He was a fine athlete, lacking only a touch of genius, the extra drive of a great runner—such as Harold Abrahams possessed, and had to pay so heavily for in his personal life.

In June of 1924 on the sea coast south of London, the British team gathered at Broadstairs in Kent to complete its training. The thirty young athletes running in a tight pack along the beach at dusk looked like a large family of brothers, all dressed alike in white, all superbly fit and moving with a fine steady rhythm, the mud bespattering their sockless calves, their bare thighs pumping beneath soaked shorts, their fists clenched, and their faces reflecting various degrees of painful effort. They seemed almost like a tribe performing a primitive war dance as their feet plodded across the beach under the setting sun. Harold Abrahams and Eric Liddell were hardly distinguishable from the rest, except perhaps for the intensity of Harold's concentration and Eric's strange style that grew wilder as soon as the pace quickened and the pressure mounted.

A few people came to watch them, trying to spot the famous faces in the swiftly moving pack. Aubrey in the lead heard a father point out Harold to his young son as "one of the fastest men in England." Perhaps in the world, Aubrey thought. The Olympics would tell.

But what of Eric Liddell? He had beaten Harold once. Would he do it again when they ran together in Paris? Or had Harold's training with Sam Mussabini improved him so much that he would win this time?

Watching both of them, Aubrey couldn't imagine either of them losing. They both presented a picture of raw power, of profound dedication, such as Aubrey had never seen before in anyone. He had thought it unique to Harold, but Liddell had it, too, in his own very different way. Aubrey was impressed again by the strange contrast between the two great runners as they raced together in the Olympic pack along the beach—Harold more upright and determined than ever, his profile glowering as if trying to scare opponents into defeat, and Eric Liddell, stockier and more loosely built, with calm, open Celtic features, as serene as if he were running by himself. Yet there was a strange similarity not only in the sense of their extraordinary drive but in their bearing among other people. Unconsciously they carried themselves with a certain remoteness, as if aware how much their unique gifts set them apart.

The tension steadily mounted as the day for leaving Paris grew nearer. Nervous practical jokes increased. Andy organized a mock cricket match in the ballroom of the Carlton Hotel, where the British team was quartered, as the weather was unseasonably wet. It helped to release some of the team's nervous energy at a time when the weather kept them indoors. Then there was a rush to send off picture postcards or even long letters back home, describing the young athletes' deepest feelings to parents, wives, or girl friends.

Aubrey's parents had been no more enthusiastic than Eric Liddell's sister, Jennie, about the Olympic Games. He tried to explain what competing in the Games meant to young athletes like him. "I'm sorry you and Pa are disappointed that I should be letting the Olympic Games interfere with my studies," he wrote to his mother, "but I'm going on with them just the same. If you were my age, with a chance to *win* the world championship in Paris, you'd be just as big a fool as I am. By the way, it's awfully kind of Pa to finance me here in spite of my idiocy. It's marvellous for esprit de corps. Most of the chaps have managed to get down from Cambridge for a visit to support us."

Aubrey added: "Harold's here—as intense as ever, just as he was when I first set eyes on him at the railway station in Cambridge when we were arriving as freshmen."

Aubrey remembered how he had first seen Harold almost five years earlier, arguing with the station master! That was so typical of Harold even now. But in so many other ways he had changed. He was more mature, more self-controlled, more understanding of other people . . . and much faster.

Before leaving for Paris, the team was given a rousing send-off at a buffet lunch on the hotel terrace overlooking the flat, wet sands they had run along so many times. It was an all-male get-together organized by the British Olympic Committee. The team members were in their special blue jackets and white flannel trousers for the first time.

Champagne glasses were topped for a toast, though some of the athletes were careful only to take a token sip. Lord Birkenhead, of the British Olympic Committee, made the main speech. A bluff, burly man with more than a hint of debauchery about him, Lord Birkenhead dominated with a hard wit and a strong personality that resented opposition and usually tried to steamroll it. Although a self-made man, he was typical of the Establishment political figures who controlled British athletics. Harold listened to his speech with a cynical expression, Aubrey noted, while Eric Liddell seemed to be bored behind his polite front.

"On behalf of the Olympic Committee," said Lord Birkenhead, "may I welcome you all!"

Loud, hearty cheers came from many of the athletes, though Aubrey noticed neither Harold nor Eric Liddell seemed very enthusiastic.

"Seriously though, gentlemen," Lord Birkenhead continued, "you are the favored few. You constitute what is without doubt the most powerful athletic force ever to leave these shores. You are to face the world's best, brown and yellow, white and black, all young and ardent as yourselves, fleet of foot and strong of limb, from every civilized nation on the face of the earth. I am in no doubt whatsoever you will acquit yourselves honorably and with distinction. Good luck to you all!''

Next came the public departure at London's Victoria Station, where a large gathering of reporters and photographers descended on the team for pictures and interviews. The athletes were dressed for the occasion in suits and ties, with walking sticks and umbrellas, but this formal attire couldn't hide their youthful excitement.

Lord Birkenhead acted as master of ceremonies and chief spokesman. He was questioned especially about the big American team that was on its way across the Atlantic and was considered the top favorite to come away with the most medals.

"The Americans have prepared themselves specially, some might say too specially, to gain success," Lord Birkenhead said. "But we feel we may, in our own unsophisticated way, have their match."

There was a low cheer from some of his listeners.

"They do have a number of men who rank as world beaters . . . ''

A rumble of agreement followed.

" . . . but this contest is in Europe and not the rarefied climes of the United States. Parisian conditions are bound to be more robust, more combative and certainly more cavalier. And in Abrahams . . .''

Harold's dark eyes lit up as he wondered what was coming.

"Liddell . . ."

Eric showed no reaction, as if completely unconcerned.

". . . and Lindsay, we have the men to give them a run for their money."

Harold half-smiled, more at ease, but then went back to his brooding, already running the Olympic race in his mind. This time he wouldn't look for Liddell!

Suddenly there was a commotion in the watching crowd, and Andy arrived with a group of servants carrying what amounted to a mountain of luggage.

"Andy," said Aubrey, grinning, "It's 'Paree' we're going to, not Peru."

"I'm a noble, remember," said the handsome young Lord. "This is a privilege of the privileged."

He glanced round.

"Seen Harold?" he asked Aubrey.

"Not yet, but he must be somewhere here. This is one train he's not going to miss."

A loudspeaker blared an announcement that the Golden Arrow train was about to leave.

"Where is Harold?" said Aubrey, beginning to grow anxious, staring in all directions.

Harold wasn't far away. He had gone to the station's snack-bar, to have a farewell drink with Sam Mussabini.

"I only wish you could come along with the team, Sam," he told the little trainer, who was chewing on his usual cigar. "I tried to get you a place, but—"

"I know, I'm *persona non grata*," said Sam, unconcerned. "There's too many old buffers' bunions to tread on. Do you feel ready, Mr. Abrahams? That's the main thing."

"As ready as I'll ever be."

They shook hands warmly.

"Sam, how can I ever thank you?"

"Get to the tape first, that's the only way."

"I'll do my best." At the door, Harold said quickly, "Be seeing you then."

Sam winked. "In a couple of days."

The Golden Arrow train took the team as far as Dover. From there they would cross the English Channel in a few hours to France.

About to board the cross-channel steamer, Eric heard his name called out by a familiar voice.

It was Sandy McGrath.

"Sandy, you've not come all the way from Scotland just to see me off?"

"No, I have not," replied Sandy with a broad grin. "I'm seeing myself off."

"You're what?"

"Get on the steamer, will ye? It'll go without you."

"But, man, I can't have a personal coach with me. It's not allowed."

"I'm not your coach, I'm your valet. And I've got my ticket. D'you want me to waste it?"

"No!"

"Spoken like a true Scot. Up you get, go on."

86

A reporter yelled out as Eric and Sandy were half way up the gangplank. "Mr. Liddell, what d'you think your chances are against Abrahams?"

"I'll do my best," replied Eric quietly. He had answered the question a hundred times already. "I can do no less."

The reporter shouted another question above the noise, "What about Sunday? Do you think you can beat the Yanks?"

Eric was only half paying attention, his mind partly on boarding the steamer. Sandy pushed him in away from the reporter. But the meaning of the reporter's question suddenly registered.

"Sandy, that reporter—"

"Now don't forget, Eric, if they ask any questions, I'm not your coach."

"Sandy, did that reporter say *Sunday?*"

Harold pushed his way toward the dockside barrier, carrying his suitcases. Reporters and photographers tried to stop him, but he had no time to answer any of their questions. Then he saw her—his lovely Sybil, even more beautiful than he remembered. She had come to see him off. He rushed to her. It was the first time he had seen her since he had asked her to stay away from his training."I came to wish you luck," she said simply.

He stared at her and touched her face. "I'm glad."

"And I understand, Harold. I wanted you to know

that. I'll be here . . . when you come back."

Harold kissed Sybil quickly and dashed for the steamer, which had already sounded its departure horn.

She watched him until he waved and disappeared, shouting to him, "Good luck, Harold! Make sure you win!" She added to herself, "For both of us." Reporters gathered round, asking questions, but she ignored them. Her relationship with Harold was their own business. But she felt encouraged. It wasn't all over. She had been very uncertain whether to go against his wishes and show up, but he had said he was "glad." She could still feel his touch, his kiss. He had missed her as much as she had missed him. If only he could win in Paris . . . then he *would* come back to her. She dreaded to think what might happen if he lost.

It was a bluff, windy day as the crowded steamer headed for the French coast across the English Channel.

Harold passed Eric on the top deck, but the quiet Scot, his great rival, didn't return his greeting. Eric seemed totally preoccupied. Was the Olympic tension beginning to affect even him? Harold wondered.

Harold was only partially correct. It wasn't the Olympic races that worried Eric. If it came to that, he would do his best and hope that would be good enough to win. What worried him was whether he could run at all. Sandy had confirmed that the heats for the 100 meters were to be held on the Sunday after the opening ceremony. The semi-finals and the final would follow a couple of days later.

But Sandy refused to accept the seriousness of the situation.

"Och, come on, Eric. It's only a heat. Does it make all *that* difference?"

"Aye," Eric said flatly. "All the difference in the world."

Obey Your Parents

Children, obey your parents in the Lord, for this is right. "Honor your father and mother" — which is the first commandment with a promise — "that it may be well with you and that you may enjoy long life on the earth."

Ephesians 6:1–3, NIV

The Lord's instruction to all His creatures is to respect and honor the parents whom He has placed over us. This is a commandment, one of the laws that govern our universe. Whether one is a child of God or a distant creation, His laws are still the governing force of our universe. In honoring and loving our parents there also is a profound, innate need to gain their approval. It is as though, if we gain their approval, we have somehow secured the Lord's as well. Harold gives us another glimpse of his character in seeking his mother's approval of Sybil. Mrs. Abrahams knows her son very well and courageously expresses her concern over a non-Jewish bride-to-be. It is admirable that she is so forthright while possibly jeopardizing their future relationship as mother and son. Wisely, Harold accepts his mother's counsel concerning his final preparation for the Olympics; essentially, he agrees to separate himself from Sybil during this time in order to concentrate fully on his goal of a gold medal.

Sybil is not at all pleased with Harold's new marching orders. In fact, she confides to Earl Lindsay — Andy — her concern that Harold's future plans may not, after all, include her. She anxiously questions Andy for his opinion and insight into the matter. Andy reveals a perceptiveness about Harold and assures Sybil she has not a thing to worry about — that while Andy's and Harold's attitudes about achieving excellence vary broadly, Andy is quite certain of Harold's love for Sybil. Sybil then realizes that Harold's present actions are not at all unlike those after his loss to Eric when he wanted to dismiss her from his presence. When Sybil later sends Harold off to the Paris Olympics, she has regained her composed assurance that Harold indeed loves her. She encourages him to win the gold medal for both of their sakes and assures Harold that, win or lose, she will be waiting for him upon his return.

Aubrey's observations of his Olympic teammates, Harold Abrahams and Eric Liddell, reveal the uniqueness of these two individuals. Unconsciously, they carry themselves with a certain remoteness, as if aware how much their special gifts set them apart. Both of these runners present a picture of raw power and profound dedication such as Aubrey has never seen.

Soon, however, Eric's religious principles receive a severe test. After the many long hours of preparation, he is finally about to realize one of his greatest dreams — that of participating in the Paris Olympics — when he learns that the 100-meter preliminaries are to be run on a Sunday. Will he compromise on his principle of keeping the Sabbath holy and free from athletic competition? Or will he yield to his dreams of Olympic glory? Sandy attempts to make light of the situation while Eric assures him that a Sunday preliminary heat is not in his plans.

Questions for Reflection and Discussion

1. A person who listens to God establishes fundamental principles. What principles are essential to your life?
2. Harold and Eric are unique members of the British Olympic team. They are different in character, yet similar in purpose. How are you set apart as an individual for Christ? What gifts operate through you to make you different? How can you improve your witness for the Lord Jesus Christ?

3. Sybil risks her relationship with Harold by appearing at dockside to send him off, to encourage him and to express her love. Do you have that kind of love that risks relationships for the sake of someone's salvation or a friend's further growth in Christ?

4. Harold alludes to the remote idea that he could possibly live without a gold medal. Could his public, his fans, let him live without it? Do you allow your family, your friends, to be themselves, however short they fall of your expectations? What kinds of pressure do we place on one another in our immediate families or the family of God? Where is the balance between pressure and encouragement?

5. One of Eric's principles is to "keep God's Sabbath day holy." If questioned as to your most fundamental principles, what would they be? Would you be willing to boldly stand by them as Eric did when he was challenged?

6. Sybil is called to the background, so to speak, as Harold completes his training for the Olympics. She must decrease her presence, and in doing so, shows her depth of maturity. How have you been asked to decrease your presence, to think of someone else before yourself? Have you followed through? What or who has been a help to you in doing this?

7. Eric honors his parents' way of life. The challenge to run on a Sunday will do one of two things for Eric: it will either be a building block to strengthen his character or a stumbling block to undermine it. How do you use challenges in your life? Do you stumble and fall? Or do you allow the Holy Spirit to encourage you in new growth? Tell about a time when you were challenged in this manner.

7

The few hours between Dover and the French port of Calais passed quickly thanks above all to Harold Abrahams. To everyone's surprise, Harold provided the entertainment on board the Channel steamer. The solitary runner in training now became a boisterous pianist and singer, leading a crowd of fellow athletes and passengers in his favorite Gilbert and Sullivan songs.

Watching Harold at the keyboard, all cares apparently forgotten in the exhilaration of the music, Aubrey wondered if he were deliberately distracting himself about the coming Olympic trials by filling in time with music and song as he used to do at Cambridge between exams. But Aubrey himself wasn't in the mood for such heartiness, so he left Harold and the chorus gathered round him to sit in a quiet corner. Taking out a writing pad from his jacket pocket, he began a letter to his family.

"I wish you could see, Ma, the wonderful spirit abroad now that we've left England," he wrote. "Harold on the piano with his beloved Gilbert and Sullivan. We're all relaxing and laughing and chatting about anything—anything but running. We're here for Britain and we know it. I'm here for you, Mum, you and Pa. I hope I do you proud. There's not a chap amongst us who isn't ready to burst his heart for all we've left behind."

But one member of the team was even more reflective than Aubrey. Eric kept totally to himself. He stood alone on the deck staring out across the Channel hour after hour, tormented by indecision. He remembered Jennie's warning that he had to choose between his running and his religious beliefs. "Your mind's not with us any more, Eric." He remembered his father's warning that compromise was the work of the Devil. And he recalled, too, how he himself had warned the two boys outside the church in the Highlands about kicking a ball on a Sunday. Now he had to practice what he'd preached. But it was a momentous decision, undoing all the training of the last few years.

The other members of the team soon noticed Eric's depressed mood, for he was usually so pleasant and encouraging. He was one of the main hopes of the team and so everyone was concerned, but nobody dared to inquire directly. Finally Aubrey talked to Sandy McGrath and soon the news was all round the steamer: Eric had decided not to run.

Nobody believed it at first, but then when Aubrey explained Eric's reason, it fitted the character of the man. Eric was greatly respected for his quiet integrity. The team as a whole took the news very badly. It might cost them a gold medal. Harold responded more gloomily than anyone. He would miss the chance of running against Liddell again—and beating him. A compromise must be worked out. Where was Lord Birkenhead? That was what those Olympic politicians were for. . . .

They all waited for Eric to make his formal announcement. White-faced but calm, he went to Lord Birkenhead's cabin.

"Won't run?" roared Lord Birkenhead. "Won't *run*?" He was almost apoplectic. "What d'you mean, man, you won't run?"

Eric faced him without flinching.

"I mean, sir, I *can't* run."

"If you're fit, sir, you can run. What you mean is you *won't*."

"Aye, sir," Eric replied quietly, "I won't."

"In God's name, why?"

"The 100-meter heats, they're on Sunday, and I won't run, not on the Lord's Day."

Lord Birkenhead was amazed. He was completely unused to such an open expression of faith. He looked at Eric, at his steady unblinking gaze, at his composure . . . and prepared his attack. Liddell had to be reasoned out of it.

"You mean it, don't you?" he said sympathetically.

"Aye! I do!"

"Then sit down, man, sit down. Let's talk about this. I like a man who means what he says. It brings the best out of me. Do you find that yourself?"

"Aye! I do."

"Good." He opened a cocktail cabinet.

"No, thanks. I don't drink."

"Mind if I do?"

"I'm not sure I'm entitled to mind."

"Damn right you're not," roared Lord Birkenhead, pouring himself a big tumbler of scotch. "Now when did you decide upon this course of action?"

"Today. When I discovered the heat was on the Sabbath, the decision was made for me."

"And didn't the possibility occur to you before? Knowing the Continentals, knowing the French? They're capable of anything."

"No, sir, I never thought of it. The idea of running on the Sabbath doesn't come into my thinking."

Lord Birkenhead studied Eric's serious face. "No, I don't suppose it does." He drank his scotch thoughtfully. "So you want to pull out, eh? Reject your country and your king. It's an awful step you're contemplating, Liddell. Yourself and Abrahams are our key men, you realize that. The whole of Britain will be watching you, and I'm not sure they'll understand. I'm not sure that *I* understand."

Eric looked down at his shoes, his running feet. "I'm not sure that *I* understand." His head went back as it did when he was running. "I've run, driven myself, and run and run again for three whole years, just to be on this ship. I gave up rugby, my work has suffered. I've even deeply hurt someone I hold very dear. Because, I told myself, if I won, I would win for God—it was His will. And now I find myself sitting here destroying it all, with a couple of words. But I *have* to. To run would be against God's law."

Lord Birkenhead was moved by Eric's simple frankness. He brooded over his scotch. Harold and his exuberant chorus could be heard singing in the distance.

"My boy, as things stand, you must not run," he said slowly. "My grandfather was like you and he was a miner, even more pigheaded. He used to say, 'A man's faith is a man's self. He is what he stands for. If he compromises that, he risks his entire salvation.' It's a noble position to take, but a dangerous and sometimes heathen one."

"In what way?"

"He drove my father from the house. He was seventeen. And do you know what for? Skating on the Sabbath!" He let Eric think about that for a moment, then he told him firmly in the tone of a commanding officer, "I want you to hold your fire for a while, son, and leave this to me, will you? Say nothing to anyone. Once it gets out, our so-called patriotic press would dine on you nightly with relish. So wait until we get to Paris. Let me talk to the Froggies. I'm not without a certain pull. And after all we fought the war together. They do owe us something."

"I don't understand," Eric said.

"They're not a very principled lot, the French, but faced with a stand like yours, one never knows. I might get through. I might just possibly persuade them."

"To do what?"

"To shift that bloody heat of yours to another day, of course."

On arrival in Paris at the Gare du Nord, one of the main railway depots in the French capital, Eric tried to avoid reporters, but it was impossible. He and Harold Abrahams were the main attractions. Harold seemed to enjoy thoroughly all the attention; he had a flair for the big occasion. But Eric was nervous, on edge in case he was forced into comment or let slip news of his dilemma. Lord Birkenhead tried to help by dominating the foreign journalists in his loud, badly pronounced French.

For many of the young athletes, Paris was a new world, and they left the busy train station wide-eyed, gazing about them, excited, elated, but also apprehensive about what lay ahead. They had to take some gold medals back to England and their best prospects were Abrahams and Liddell, but now Liddell's availability depended on persuading the French to change the order of the races, and that was not likely at this late stage.

A *Paris Match* reporter tried to corner Eric about the 100 meters—had he heard some gossip?—but Lord Birkenhead stepped between them, waving his arms.

"Everyone aboard the bus, please. No more questions. There's a press reception arranged for later."

Eric walked quickly to the bus and his fellow athletes made way for him. The French reporter watched curiously. He sensed something was wrong. Eric was being given special treatment. The whole team seemed to be trying to express support for him in his predicament. He sat with his face to the window, thinking that if Lord Birkenhead failed to reach an agreement with the French, he might as well go home to Scotland.

Be Still and Wait

Trust in the Lord, and do good;
   so you will dwell in the land and enjoy security.
Take delight in the Lord,
   and he will give you the desires of your heart.
Commit your way to the Lord;
   trust in him, and he will act.
He will bring forth your vindication as the light,
   and your right as the noonday.
Be still before the Lord, and wait patiently for him;
   fret not yourself over him who prospers in his way. . . ."
Psalm 37:3–7, RSV

In Philippians, the Apostle Paul shares his confidence that He who has begun a good work in you will complete it on that day that Jesus Christ returns. It is the same kind of confidence most of these athletes on the British Olympic team must have felt as they frolicked across the English Channel. They needed this time to relax, to forget the seriousness of the adventure—all, that is, except Eric, who was questioning just exactly what he was doing on this ship, going to an Olympics in which he surely wouldn't be competing. He remembers what his father said in his sermon—that compromise was of the Devil—and his sister, Jennie, who insisted that he would have to choose between his running and his religious beliefs. Doubt filled his mind. Why did it have to come to this? Why me? Haven't I heard clearly from you, Lord? Is this running just my desire?

At moments such as this, the Christian has more at stake than meets the eye: dying of self, practicing what we have preached, and the way we really let Jesus carry our burdens—our witness to others. Christians are not eliminated from the test decisions of life, but they do have the promise that Jesus is there to help lead them. Eric must have felt this as he wrestled with his dilemma.

When Eric meets with Lord Birkenhead, the latter belittles Eric's decision to put God before king and country. Lord Birkenhead admits to a lack of understanding about Eric's decision, but avoids confrontation by suggesting a possible solution after conferring with the French Olympic committee.

Will Eric's uncompromising attitude hold up under pressure from the British Olympic committee? Will he opt for human adulation and immediate approval and choose to run, thinking that "only" God will be hurt? Or will he remain true to his principles and honor the God of this universe?

Questions for Reflection and Discussion

1. Lord Birkenhead was amazed at the standard Eric had chosen to bear. Tell about some people who amaze you at the way they stand for Jesus. What makes them modern-day Eric Liddells?

2. Lord Birkenhead comments that the whole of Britain will be looking at Eric: "We are surrounded by so great a cloud of witnesses . . ." (Hebrews, 12:1). How do we keep our eyes on Jesus in the midst of severe testing of our principles?

3. The British team rally to Eric's predicament. How do we as Christians rally for one another? Do we allow our wounded Christians to die, or do we run to their aid with encouragement and with support through prayer?

8

The modern Olympics, founded in 1896, were inspired by French nobleman Baron Pierre de Courbertin, who thought the Olympic Games of Ancient Greece embodied "the noble and chivalrous character of athletics" and therefore should be revived in all their glory.

But the Baron was also a realist and understood that modern international sporting events couldn't be free of politics. He warned therefore that the modern Olympics "can occasion the most noble passions or the most vile."

Although 45 nations were competing in Paris, the Eighth Olympiad was destined to be remembered for the "most noble passions" of a few individual athletes, who found there the fulfillment of their dreams.

But as the opening ceremony approached, Eric's participation seemed very much in doubt, and the most eagerly awaited athletes came from across the Atlantic. The Americans had sent a team of nearly four hundred, hoping to establish their athletic superiority in the post-war world of the Twenties. They were expected to take almost all the medals in the track and field events.

Harold, Andy and Aubrey went to a movie house in Paris to watch the powerful American team arriving at the French port of Le Havre. The silent newsreel film showed the liner *America* with its huge sign "American Olympic Team" and a 200-meter cork track laid out on the promenade deck where the team had practiced in mid-Atlantic. A big French crowd welcomed the smiling Americans.

"That's Charlie Paddock," murmured Harold, eyeing the cinema screen, "and Fitch and Taylor." These were the faces he had studied with Sam Mussabini. He knew them and their records by heart. There were the men he had to beat—these men and Eric Liddell.

"My God, look at the size of Paddock," said Aubrey. "He's a giant."

Harold was silent, unhearing, an image of the big smiling American burning into his brain. He *must* beat this man.

"There's Jackson Scholtz," said Andy.

"He's more my size," said Harold, "but mean with it."

"Never seen a meaner," Aubrey told him. "You've got your hands full there, Harold."

"Yes, a real battle on your hands," added Andy. "But that brings out the best in you, Harold."

Harold smiled grimly. It was true. He was never more himself than in a race. And this 100 meter sprint—a mere ten seconds out of a whole lifetime—would be the toughest contest he would ever be in.

Paddock was shown in the newsreel acknowledging the cheers with his arms clasped over his head, a massive man, cheerful and very confident. The caption on the silent movie screen read: "Charles H. Paddock, *l'homme le plus vite du monde*."

"The fastest man in the world," translated Harold.

His tone made Aubrey glance quickly at him. Harold was irritated at all the fuss made of the Americans. That would be good for him, stoking up even more that incredible drive of his.

When the American team reached Paris, Harold and the others went to observe them at their training camp, where the Americans continued a highly disciplined routine right up to the opening day of the Games. They were regimented by merciless trainers, who tried to keep the whole team in top mental and physical condition. Army basic training was no more rigorous and all-demanding. "Welcome to the Bastille prison," Paddock told some visitors.

Harold recalled the Cambridge criticisms of him for hiring a professional coach. What would the Cambridge dons say about the Americans who had a whole team trained by professionals? Truly they were a formidable lot.

Harold had found a room for Sam Mussabini near the Olympic stadium and met him at the station on arrival to help him with his bags. Sam was delighted the room overlooked the stadium, for it would be as close as he would get to the Games. The British Olympic Committee had refused to invite him and he thought it more diplomatic to keep behind the scenes to save Harold from further criticism.

Harold had completely fitted out Sam's room for their

final training sessions. There was a massage table in the center, an array of rubbing oils and towels, and pictures of Eric Liddell and the Americans, Paddock and Scholtz, as constant reminders of the challenge Harold faced.

"This will give us quiet, lad," said Sam enthusiastically. "It's tip-top, Mr. Abrahams. You've done a grand job."

"You have everything you need?"

"Everything. If we don't win now, we never will."

The opening ceremony for the Eighth Olympiad was held in perfect summer weather in the Colombes Stadium on Saturday, July 5, 1924. A crowd of about sixty thousand watched the French President, introduced by Baron de Courbertin, officially declare the Games open in a bright, noisy carnival atmosphere. The Olympic torch was lit and the Olympic flag with its five symbolic circles was hoisted to the music of the French national anthem, the rousing *Marseillaise*. Artillery salvos crashed out a salute and the air was suddenly full of pigeons taking the news to the outside world.

The standards dipped and, to the singing of a Czech choir, Georges Andre, the famous French Olympic hurdler, mounted the dais overlooking the field of contest. Turning to the assembled athletes, with right hand raised, he read aloud the Olympic oath in French and English: "We swear that we come to the Eighth Olympiad animated by a respect for the regulations which govern it, and desirous of participating for the honor of our countries and the glory of sport.''

In the crowd of athletes, right hands raised at arms' length, Eric and Harold stood close together, Eric solemn and troubled, Harold smiling proudly.

Four French military bands marched through the Marathon Gate and around the main track. The British team, the men in white felt or straw hats, blue blazers and white trousers, the women in cream pleated skirts, were led round by the pipes of the 2nd Queen's Own Cameron Highlanders, which greatly moved Eric and made him nostalgic for his home. He wished he had left for Scotland already to avoid any last minute pleas from Lord Birkenhead.

The Games began well for the British team. Andrew Lindsay, serious for once but with the same casual easy style, came second in the hurdles, winning a silver medal. Harold and Aubrey carried Andy shoulder-high through the cheering crowd, and Lord Birkenhead slapped him on the back and offered him a cigar. Then the Prince of Wales, who was to become King Edward the Eighth and later abdicate to marry Mrs. Wallis Simpson, joined in with his personal congratulations.

The British Olympic Association that night gave a reception and dance in honor of the teams from the British Empire countries. Lord Birkenhead introduced the Prince of Wales to the assembled guests.

''The Royal Benediction no less,'' remarked Harold sardonically, as he observed the Prince's progress around the vast ballroom.

"The chap's invaluable," replied Andy. "We couldn't do without him. He's here to show us what may be done and more essentially what may not be."

Harold watched closely as the Prince and Lord Birkenhead retired to the back of the ballroom for a private discussion. It was obvious whom they were talking about, for they kept eyeing Eric Liddell, who was standing alone, looking troubled and detached from the party around him. The same forces that tried to teach me my place in society, Harold thought, are now about to try to teach Eric Liddell his place. What had Andy said about the Prince of Wales—he's here to show us what *may* be done. No, it was more like what must be done. Eric Liddell was about to be given a lesson in blind obedience, poor fellow.

Lord Birkenhead left the Prince and slowly made his way over to Eric.

"Ah, Liddell, I was afraid you weren't here."

"To be honest, I'd rather not be, sir," said Eric with his usual frankness.

"Nonsense, my boy," replied Lord Birkenhead. "Do you good. Take you out of yourself a bit." He paused, trying to sound casual. "The Prince would like to meet you."

"Och, no, sir," Eric protested, knowing what this meant.

"He expressed a particular desire to make your acquaintance, Liddell. He considers you and Abrahams 'the linch pins of our aspirations.' Those were his very words."

"It wouldn't be right, sir. I mean, things being as they are. . . ."

Lord Birkenhead said impatiently, "Liddell, he's your future king. Are you refusing to shake his hand? Does your arrogance extend that far?"

Eric flushed. "My arrogance, sir," he replied, "extends just as far as my conscience demands."

"Fine, but I hope it's wise enough to allow for maneuver."

Eric nodded. He didn't wish to be rude. "I'd be honored to meet the Prince."

"Splendid." Lord Birkenhead relaxed at once, smiling warmly. He put an arm round Eric's shoulders. "I'll take you to him now."

Watching them walk out of the ballroom, Harold Abrahams thought *there goes Daniel into the lion's den.* Liddell would have to be very strong to withstand such Royal pressure.

Eric was taken into a private sittingroom where the Prince of Wales, smoking a cigarette, and the members of the British Olympic Committee were awaiting him.

"Your Royal Highness," said Lord Birkenhead very grandly, "may I present Mr. Eric Liddell."

The Prince rose and shook hands. "Delighted, Liddell, delighted. I saw you play rugby for Scotland. Depressed me no end. Ran in a couple of tries from your own half, I remember. Well, nice to have you on the same side at last. Excellent effort of Lindsay's, don't you think?"

"He did well, sir," replied Eric. "He did, indeed."

"An example to us all," said the Prince.

Lord Birkenhead introduced Eric to the other men. The Duke of Sutherland, President of the British Olympic Association, a slim nervous man, gave Eric a cordial handshake. But the chairman, Lord Cadogan, with a grim bulldog face, ignored Eric's hand and scowled at him.

"Please be seated, Eric," said Lord Birkenhead, gesturing to an upright chair in the center. Eric sat down, feeling like a defendant on trial.

"Cigar?" asked Lord Birkenhead genially. "No, of course you don't. Nor drink." He glanced at the others. "Such is the resolution of the young man you have before you, gentlemen."

The Duke of Sutherland said politely, "Lord Birkenhead has advised us as to your attitude toward your participation in the hundred meters heat, Liddell. Or would your *non*-participation be more accurate?"

Eric, sitting upright, said uncomfortably, "It would, sir, yes."

"We were also consulted as to the proper manner in which to approach the French."

"Something we just can't allow to happen," grunted Lord Cadogan, staring unpleasantly at Eric. "Going cap in hand to the Frogs, of all people. Simply out of the question."

The Prince added more gently, "A simple matter of national dignity, Liddell. Being a patriot, I'm sure you understand."

"Well, I must say, sir," replied Eric, "I felt it was an impractical suggestion from the start."

"Then why didn't you damn well say so, man?" snapped Lord Birkenhead. "As an athlete, you must value economy of effort."

Eric said quickly, "I wanted to run. I was desperate enough to try anything."

The Prince, the Duke, and the two Lords exchanged quick glances.

"So," said the Duke of Sutherland, "all that being understood, we decided to invite you in for a chat, to see if there is any way that we can resolve the situation."

Lord Cadogan said impatiently, "There's only one way to resolve the situation, and that's for this young man to change his mind and run."

"Don't state the obvious, Cadogan," said the Prince. "We've to explore ways in which we can help this young man to reach that decision."

Eric said simply but with great firmness, "I'm afraid there are no ways, sir." The others stared at him. "I cannot run on the Sabbath and that's final. I intended to confirm this with Lord Birkenhead tonight, even before you called me before this inquisition of yours."

"Don't be impertinent, Liddell," snapped Lord Cadogan.

"The impertinence lies, sir, with those who seek to influence a man to deny his beliefs."

"On the contrary, Liddell," said Lord Birkenhead. "We're appealing to your beliefs in your country and your King . . . to your loyalty to them."

"Hear! Hear!" barked Lord Cadogan. "In my day, it was King first and God after."

"Yes," said the Duke of Sutherland quickly. "And the recent Great War to end all wars bitterly proved your point." He gave Lord Cadogan an icy look, silencing him.

"God made countries and God makes kings and the rules by which they govern," said Eric. "Those rules say the Sabbath is His and I for one intend to keep it that way."

A brief silence ensued. Then the Prince spoke up. Surely Eric would listen to him.

"Mr. Liddell, you're a child of your race as I am. We share a common heritage, a common bond, a common loyalty. There are times when we're asked to make sacrifices in the name of that loyalty. Without them, our allegiance is worthless. As I see it, for you, this is such a time."

Eric bowed his head and said in a low voice, "Sir, God knows I love my country. But I can't make that sacrifice."

Lord Cadogan snorted with anger. The Duke of Sutherland turned his back on Eric and stood staring down into the room's old fireplace. The Prince, irritated, lit a cigarette. Eric was left isolated and was about to leave.

Suddenly there was an interruption.

A uniformed attendant announced, "Lord Lindsay."

Andy hurried in, glanced quickly round, and went and stood by Eric. The Prince and the others gave him friendly looks. Not only was the young Lord one of them, an aristocrat himself, but he had won a silver medal.

"Your Highness, Cadogan, Gentlemen," he said, "I do apologize for barging in like this. The fact is I'm fully aware of Eric's dilemma, and I wonder if I could be so bold as to suggest a possible solution."

"Do," said Lord Cadogan.

"Another day, another race," Andy replied.

"What the devil's that supposed to mean?" growled Lord Cadogan.

111

"It's quite simple, as a matter of fact, sir. The 400 meters, it's on Thursday. I've already got my medal, so why don't you let Eric take my place in the 400 meters?"

"I think that's a splendid idea," said the Duke of Sutherland.

"Can we allow him to change events at such short notice?" inquired Lord Cadogan. "That's a matter for the committee."

"We are the committee," snapped Lord Birkenhead. "I think it's a very good idea, Lindsay." He looked at the Prince. "David?"

The Prince smiled. "All those in favor say, 'Aye.' "

"Aye," cried the others.

The Prince glanced at Eric, who had said nothing. "Liddell?"

Eric turned to Andy.

"Andy, I . . . " It embarrassed him that Andy was sacrificing his own chance for another Olympic medal.

Andy grinned. "A pleasure, old chap, just to see you run."

Eric decided he couldn't turn down such a sporting offer. "Then 'Aye' it is."

He gripped Andy's hand, trying to express his gratitude. He would be able to run after all. He gave a sigh of relief. It would be his last chance before leaving for missionary work in China. Perhaps it would be the last race he would ever run.

Lord Birkenhead whispered to the Duke of Sutherland, "Thank God for Lindsay, George. I thought the lad had us beaten."

"He did have us beaten," the Duke said quietly. "And thank God he did."

"I don't follow, George."

"The *'lad,'* as you call him, is a true man of principle and a true athlete. His speed is a mere extension of his life, its force. We sought to sever his running from himself."

"For his country's sake."

"No sake is worth that," said the Duke, "least of all a guilty national pride."

The headlines were soon across the world:

ATHLETE: I WON'T RUN ON SUNDAY
GOD BEFORE KING
LIDDELL ABANDONS SHIP: SCOT RUNS FROM 100 METERS—
ABRAHAMS TO FACE YANKS ALONE
LINDSAY MAKES WAY FOR LIDDELL

The public reaction was mixed. Some people thought Eric must be a fanatic; others praised him as a man of principle, including most of his teammates. His fellow athletes soon heard how he had stood up to everybody, even the Prince of Wales. But thanks to the self-sacrifice of Andrew Lindsay, Eric would run later in the week. It was a popular solution with them all except Harold Abrahams.

I've lost the chance of revenge, was Harold's first

thought when he heard that Eric Liddell was definitely out of the 100 meters. Liddell and he would now run in different races against the Americans. Yet later, when Harold had more time to think calmly about the change, he decided it was more satisfactory than if Eric Liddell had given in to all the official pressure. He and Liddell had more in common than he had thought. Neither of them was willing to compromise.

Simply Say "Yes" or "No"

> Let what you say be simply "Yes" or "No"; anything more than this comes from evil.
>
> Matthew 5:37, RSV

The Olympics is the ultimate in athletic competition. It is second to none, duplicated by no other sporting event in the world.

The 1964 Tokyo Olympics were the first in which I personally competed. For me, as a schoolboy of seventeen, the entire experience was absolutely euphoric. From the moment I stepped off the plane in Tokyo, I knew I was in for something very special. The Olympic village hummed with various different languages; the physical features of the competitors were as varied as the countries from which they hailed. Each of us held in our hearts a sense of great anticipation, knowing that we had yet to run what for most of us would be our finest race yet.

Much as Harold, Aubrey, and Andy went to the movie theater to view their American competition, I walked through the Olympic village seeking out my competition, sizing them up, and determining what my chances were against them.

Eric, however, does not share in any of this pre-Olympic anticipation, still wondering how he had erred in his decision to run and wanting to return home to Scotland. Soon he will be called to give his final decision to the British Olympic committee.

When seated before this prestigious group, Eric is demeaningly challenged as to why he would dare put God before the king. We know that there is no temptation that befalls man for which God will not provide an avenue of escape. There is no evidence that Eric would compromise his stand, not even a little. On the contrary, it was the British Olympic committee that had to marvel at Eric's strength of character. Indeed, he was a man of astounding principle, unyielding and immovable. He showed these men that his talent for running was merely a byproduct of his great love for God.

A solution, however, is provided for everyone involved when Lord Lindsay nobly offers to give up his chance for a second Olympic medal and let Eric run in his place in the 400-meter dash.

Unfortunately, Harold realizes that his chance for revenge has been lost. He will not have the opportunity to beat Eric Liddell at his own race of 100 meters. In fact, he will never have another chance; this will be Eric's last race before he returns to the missionary field. What frustration Harold must have felt!

Questions for Reflection and Discussion

1. In this day of prevailing greed, of getting all one can get for oneself, it is refreshing and encouraging to see how God uses Lord Lindsay to fulfill His purpose for Eric. Lord Lindsay is willing to sacrifice his chance for a second Olympic medal — his rightful opportunity and not an everyday occurrence. When was the last time you heard about, thought of, or participated in such a sacrifice?

2. As Eric goes to his inquisition, Harold thinks, "There he goes, like Daniel into the lion's den." Just as God showed His faithfulness to Daniel, he did likewise for Eric and does for each of us today. Tell about one of your lion's den experiences. How did you see God's steadfastness? How did He prevail on your behalf?

3. The Duke of Sutherland recognizes that Eric's speed is simply an extension of his life, of its force. Should we separate our Monday-through-Saturday lives from our Sunday lives with Christ? Is every-

thing in your life an extension of Christ? How do you make it so?

4. A solution to Eric's dilemma was not offered until what seemed like the very last moment. Do you think his faith would have been shaken had a solution not been found? Would yours have been?

5. Romans 8:28 says that in all things God works for good with those who love Him, who are called according to His purpose. This was obviously true in Eric's case. Do you find it to be so in yours? Tell about one such instance.

9

On Sunday, while the 100-meter heats were being run, Eric Liddell preached a sermon in the Church of Scotland in the center of Paris. As he surveyed the large congregation, part of his mind kept thinking of the Olympic runners lining up and how he wished he were among them. Yet he had made the right decision. He had no doubt of that.

"My text this afternoon is taken from Isaiah, Chapter Forty," he said in a firm voice that carried through the still, silent church. " 'Behold, the nations are as a drop in the bucket and are counted as the small dust in the balance. . . .' " He thought of the Prince of Wales and the pressure he had brought to bear. " '. . . All nations before Him are as nothing. They are counted to Him less than nothing . . . and vanity. . . . He bringeth the princes to nothing; He maketh the judges of the earth as a vanity. . . .' " The starter's pistol would go off at any moment. The runners, including Harold Abrahams, would be poised ready for a fast start. " '. . . Hast thou not known? Hast thou not heard that the everlasting God, the Lord, the Creator of the ends of the earth, fainteth not, neither is weary. . . .' ''

At that moment, the starter's pistol cracked at the Olympic Stadium. Moments before, the American Charles Paddock had rocked forward deliberately and Harold, watching him, rocked with him, then realizing his mistake, quickly shifted back. But as he did so, the pistol went off. Paddock was ready and off to a great start, but Harold, conned, lost a precious moment and was left a yard behind. The power within Harold surged, giving him an agonized expression as he strained to catch Paddock.

From the church pulpit, Eric continued to read from the Old Testament: '' 'He giveth power to the faint, and to them that have no might, He increaseth strength. . . . But they that wait upon the Lord shall renew their strength. . . . They shall mount up with wings as eagles. They shall run and not be weary. . . .' ''

But weary he was. Harold couldn't gain back the yard he had lost at the start. Bitterly disappointed, he wanted to see only one person—Sam Mussabini.

"Juvenile, Mr. Abrahams," Sam snorted, furious with Harold for allowing himself to be psyched out by Paddock. "You lost your concentration like a kid." He began to massage Harold's exhausted body without saying any more. Harold lay on the table in Sam's room running the race again in his mind. It had been like the race against Liddell. He had allowed himself to be distracted. Sam was right. He had lost his concentration for one vital moment.

Aubrey Montague had run in the 3,000 meter steeplechase, had injured his knee at the top of the water jump, and had come in sixth. Looking for some consolation, he joined Harold and Sam. The little man's expert, oiled hands dug into Harold's taut muscles. The bands playing in the Olympic stadium could be heard faintly through the window. Aubrey sat down with a gloomy, defeated expression, not speaking. Harold understood Aubrey's mood from the way he felt himself. Remembering how much Aubrey had encouraged him, Harold tried to raise his friend's spirits.

"Do you remember when we first bumped into each other, old chap?" he asked softly, looking up from the massage table. "We shared a taxi, remember? You made me feel so much older, burdened, sour . . . even superior." He chuckled. "That was the miscalculation of my life. You, Aubrey, are my most complete man."

This was high praise from Harold, but Aubrey was too depressed to respond.

Harold said warmly, "You're kind, compassionate, brave. A contented man. That's your secret—contentment. I'm twenty-four and I've never known it. I'm forever in pursuit and I don't even know what it is I'm chasing. Aubrey, old chap, I'm scared. Sam and I, we've labored, rowed and bullied for this, day in, day out. You've seen us, chuckled over us, I'm sure, out in all weathers. Madmen. And for what? I was beaten by Paddock because I let him trick me. And now in one hour's time, I'll be out there again. I'll raise my eyes and look down that corridor four feet wide with ten lonely seconds to justify my whole existence. But will I? Aubrey, I've known the fear of losing, but now, I'm almost too frightened to win."

Aubrey nodded. He understood. But he could find nothing to say. He had failed his own test, coming in sixth. Would Harold fail his?

Sam Mussabini glanced at both young men as he went on kneading Harold's muscles. Aubrey, Sam thought, lacked the drive, the fire, of a great runner. The personal motivation wasn't there. Perhaps he was *too* content to have the necessary obsession with winning. But Harold had it. If he could only shut out the other runners as Eric Liddell did and just run his fastest, he would win the final. But Harold was so competitive, he always ran against the other runners, watching their progress and therefore leaving himself open to psychological games and distractions. "Concentration, Mr. Abrahams," Sam kept telling him. "Concentration will win that gold medal."

Harold had this advice in mind as he prepared for the final of the 100 meters. The atmosphere of the changing room was almost churchlike in its quietness and dedication. The Americans changed into their track suits in silence. Jackson Scholtz sat on a bench, massaging his right foot. Paddock began to undress. He was a head taller than his teammate Scholtz, a huge man. Harold sat in a corner, far from the American team. Opening his attaché case, he found a letter on top of his running clothes. It was from Sam Mussabini.

"Dear Mr. Abrahams, You must please pardon my not coming to see you run, much as I would like to do so. However, I believe and hope you will win the hundred meters. Go out determined to do your best, and don't forget to drop down at the first stride. Get well warmed up and then let the gun release you. I should use the springy old six-spike shoes. All the best of luck, from Yours Truly, Sam Mussabini.

"P.S. Please accept the charm. My old father swore by it."

Enclosed with the letter was a small gold chain and an Arab charm with an inscription from the Koran cut out in it. Harold slipped the charm around his neck. Then he was ready.

He and Paddock entered the stadium together. The American waved to people, cheerfully confident, but Harold was self-absorbed, as if he intended to allow no distractions of any kind.

The final of the 100 meters was one of the great occasions in the Games, perhaps the most eagerly awaited event, for it was the fastest race, with several world famous athletes competing against each other.

Under pale blue skies, an excited crowd, as big as the attendance on the opening day, watched the six runners line up. An American Marine band played in honor of the four American finalists, Paddock, Scholtz, Bowman and Murchison. Harold saw the Prince of Wales and Lord Birkenhead arrive. But he shut them out of his thoughts. He shut everything out to concentrate as Sam had instructed.

Even the usually smiling, friendly Americans were now solemn-faced, into themselves, thinking of the final instructions of their coach.

Tipping his hat to the ladies, the Prince of Wales came across the grass to shake each runner's hand. He told Paddock, "Dinner for your whole team at my club when we get back to London. You win, I pay. Abrahams wins, you pay. All right?"

"Sir, you have yourself a deal."

"Done! The best of luck to you."

"And to you, too, sir," said the American runner.

The Prince moved on to Harold. "Good luck, Abrahams. Do your best. That's all we can expect."

"Thank you, sir," said Harold, trying not to let the Royal interruption affect his preparations.

The Prince gazed round the arena at the flags, the band playing loud martial music, the aggressive demonstration of patriotism and nationalism from so many sides. "Wonderful show, eh?" he said to the Duke of Sutherland.

"No, sir," the Duke replied, "I'm afraid it frightens me."

"Why?"

"I'm not here for flags and anthems, but honest human endeavor, man against man . . . an innocent ideal."

"Well?" said the Prince impatiently.

"The ideal is being swamped. Just look about you. Nations have their teeth in our Games. It's an evil evolution, but it's unstoppable and it will have to run its course."

The Prince walked away without replying.

Up in the stands, Sandy McGrath said to Eric, "No regrets you're not down there?"

"Regrets, aye," Eric replied. "Doubts, no!"

The track officials were showing the runners their lanes. Harold was between the Americans Bowman and Murchison.

"To your marks."

Harold's whole life seemed to be poised with him. He was running for final recognition, to beat the devils of prejudice, so that he could establish his individual identity, free at last. Win today, he told himself, and you put yourself beyond the petty labels and restrictions of class and religion.

"Get set."

Harold told himself, Head down. Watch the first stride. Sam's charm around his neck brought back Sam's final direction, Ignore the others. He tried to.

The starter's pistol cracked.

Harold felt the fire rise within him as he launched himself forward.

It was a perfect start.

The power surged through his whole body as he sped down his lane, the tape in the far distance.

At 25 meters, all the runners were still bunched together, going flat out, but at 50 meters, the halfway mark, the great pace began to tell. Harold's adrenalin coursed through his body and he took the lead, with Scholtz and Bowman trying to catch him. But Harold didn't look to see where they were. His mind was wholly on the tape ahead. He gained a foot, two feet, and held the lead the rest of the way. Nobody could match Harold

Abrahams that day—he was the fastest man in the world! Jackson Scholtz was second, but Charlie Paddock was unable to keep up and came in a disappointing fifth.

The great crowd roared its approval. The French President congratulated the Prince of Wales. And as British supporters tried to reach the track, a solitary figure came loping across the grass. It was Eric Liddell. Breaking away from the officials shaking his hand, Harold went to meet him.

"Well done, Harold," Eric said. "Well run!"

"Thanks, Eric."

It was unnecessary to say any more. They understood each other far beyond words.

Harold went quietly through the cheering fans to the changing room. He was strangely subdued. From his manner, no one could have guessed what the race had meant to him. He packed his bag with his usual care and precision, ignoring all the noise around him. Then he glanced at the British officials opening bottles of champagne to celebrate his great win . . . and he quietly walked out.

Aubrey Montague called after him, "Harold, come and celebrate!"

"Let him go," Andrew Lindsay said. "Can't you see the poor fella's whacked?"

"But he won!"

"Exactly. One of these days, Aubrey, you're going to win yourself. And it's pretty difficult to swallow."

In London at the Savoy Theatre, Sybil was putting the finishing touches to her make-up for *The Mikado* when a doorman knocked on the door of her dressing room.

"Mrs. Abrahams just phoned, Miss," he said, very excited. "Mr. Harold—he won. She told me to tell you *he won!*"

Sybil stood up in her excitement.

"He won? Oh, thank you, thank you for telling me."

Tears ran down through her make-up.

Harold had done it.

He had won . . . and so had she.

Harold had hoped to be the first to tell Sam, but the little trainer knew already.

He had heard the starter's pistol go off, then he had sat motionless on his bed, a glass of beer untouched, counting the ten seconds the race would last. Then he waited. It seemed far longer than ten seconds. The silence went on and on. Doubts began to creep in. Perhaps Harold had lost. Perhaps they had both failed. Slowly from the stadium came music. As was the custom, the national anthem of the winner's country was played. This time it was "God Save the King," the British national anthem. Sam stood rigidly at attention until the music stopped. There were tears in his eyes. Then he let out a yell of triumph, whipped off his hat, and punched his fist right through the crown. Harold had won! He remained still and silent until he heard footsteps on the stairs.

"We did it, Sam!"

"I know, Mr. Abrahams."

The two men embraced like a father and son, trying to express their feeling of a shared triumph.

"Let's go and get a glass of beer, Mr. Abrahams," Sam said quietly, understanding Harold's subdued mood.

Harold and Sam Mussabini sat until very late in a Paris bistro. Harold was like a man suffering from a bad hangover, and Sam tried to raise his spirits in his usual blunt way.

"You've always thought of yourself as a ruthless man, haven't you?" Sam said. "Hard. A bit of a loner, like me. But actually you're as soft as a limp pocket. And you care. You care about things that really matter. If you didn't, I wouldn't have come within a mile of you." Sam lit a cigar and puffed thoughtfully, Harold's gold medal held lovingly in his hand. "Son, d'you know who you won for out there today? Us. You and old Sam Mussabini. I've waited thirty bloody years for this, Harold!" His eyes suddenly filled with tears. "It means the world to me this, y'know." A waiter began to put the chairs on the tables. "And if all the world can do is to want to go home to bed, then they can go to hell. Because we've had today, you and me, and we've got it for keeps. Now it's out of your system. Go home to that girl of yours and start some bloody living."

Harold rose to his feet and raised his glass. He, too, was crying.

"To Sam Mussabini! The greatest trainer in the world!"

Sam stood up and they touched glasses.

"Tell the waiter," Sam said thickly, "to get some more beer."

"No, Sam," said Harold, "We're going home. We've done enough for one day."

Back at Cambridge, news of Harold Abrahams' victory reached the Master of Trinity and his friend, the Master of Caius. A butler brought in a newspaper with the headline,

ABRAHAMS TRIUMPHANT—CAIUS COLLEGE ATHLETE
WINS BLUE RIBAND AT GAMES.

"Just as I expected," said the Master of Trinity with a smile of satisfaction.

The two old dons raised their sherry glasses in tribute. "To Harold!"

He had been accepted at last.

Run the Race

> Therefore, since we are surrounded by so great a cloud of witnesses, let us also lay aside every weight, and sin which clings so closely, and let us run with perseverance the race that is set before us, looking to Jesus the pioneer and perfecter of our faith, who for the joy that was set before him endured the cross, despising the shame, and is seated at the right hand of the throne of God.
>
> *Hebrews, 12:1–2, RSV*

For a coach–athlete relationship to function properly, the coach must be completely honest. Such honesty is not always easy; often it creates a rift in the relationship.

Sam is so upset over Harold's initial loss to Paddock that he unabashedly lashes out at Harold, not concerned with how it will affect their relationship. Sam

chastizes Harold as a parent would a child who has in-
nocently walked into the street in front of an oncom-
ing car. He calls him a juvenile. All of this is intended
to get Harold's attention and cause him to learn from
his mistake. Harold's problem is his lack of confidence
in, and concentration on, his own race. Sam wants
Harold to recognize that he must run his own race and
not that of his opponent, giving no thought to the
competition, but keeping his eyes steadfastly on himself and what must be done in those ten short seconds.

Harold's lack of concentration at race time is odd,
for his private thoughts indicate that his whole existence can only be justified by winning, while a loss
would be total failure. There is no doubt about it, Harold Abrahams is an enormously intense and insecure
man.

Even in his intensity, however, we see a new dimen-
sion of Harold's character blossom. His friend Aubrey
is in dire need of encouragement after his sixth-place
finish in the steeplechase and finds it in, of all places,
Harold. Harold expresses, as best as he can, his sor-
row at Aubrey's loss. He provides Aubrey with a cos-
metic bandage by telling him that Aubrey is the most
secure man he knows.

The scene changes from Sam's apartment to the
Olympic locker room. One can feel the electricity of
pre-race competition. Imagine yourself as Harold,
preparing for the "second and last chance." With
whom would you identify? A subdued Harold as he
contemplates his place in history? A relaxed Charlie
Paddock as he comes into the stadium wearing sun-
glasses and tipping his hat to the crowd? Or Eric, as he

130

confidently sits in the stands as a spectator, having no doubts that he has made the right decision? As the starter raises his pistol and gives his command, one has the feeling that for the first time, Harold is ready mentally and physically to run the best race of his life. Contrary to previous races, he now seems to have centered his full attention towards executing what he and Sam have spent three years preparing for. Harold is so intent that he never allows himself even a quick glimpse at his competition; he knows what he has to do, and it is now or never.

When Harold crosses the finish line in victory, we sense the freedom that Harold has yearned for—a freedom from petty labels and restrictions caused by class and religion. And what could make his triumph sweeter than spontaneous congratulations from Eric Liddell, who admiringly appreciates his teammate's achievement?

We know Harold's victory is complete when Sam admonishes him to forget his running and get back to normal living, to marry Sybil and settle down. Harold has achieved his goal and received his most prized possession, a gold medal.

Questions for Reflection and Discussion

1. Eric has a principle by which he has always lived— that of keeping the Sabbath day holy. When God gives you a principle by which to live, do you expect everyone else to live by it also?
2. Sam Mussabini scolds Harold for his loss in the 100-meter dash semi-final due to his lack of concentration. Do we serve a God who likewise disciplines us

131

when we take our eyes off him or purposely lose our direction? ("The Lord chastizes those whom He loves, and He will perfect that which concerns Him.")

3. Which young man do you best identify with in this chapter, Harold, Charlie, or Eric? Why?

4. Eric spontaneously congratulates Harold on his triumph. Are you able to enjoy others' success in this spontaneous manner? Why or why not?

5. Sam recognizes in Harold the need for change. He knows that, although change is not always easy, it is necessary for growth. Do you think Harold's victory in the 100-meter race freed him to make changes in his life? Do you have a clear view of how others see you? Are you willing to be made more like Christ?

10

So it came to Eric's final race. He had held his own in the qualifying heats for the 400 meters, but several of the other runners had broken the world record. Eric was in fast company — perhaps too fast.

According to Sam Mussabini, the 400 meters, the quarter mile, was above all a test of character. "The true stamp of the quartermiler," he told Harold, "is one who can go all the way through at top pressure. Of all distances, the 400 is popularly supposed to be the most trying. It relies far less on a fast start than the 100 meters and much more on stamina and judgment."

The favorite was Horatio M. M. Fitch of Chicago, who had already broken the world record in a preliminary heat. Eric Liddell had won his heat, but in a much slower time. Nothing in his performance suggested he could beat Fitch. Perhaps he would be second and win a silver medal.

The other finalists were Imbach of Switzerland, Butler of Britain, Johnson of Canada, and Taylor of the U.S.A.

The pipes and band of The Queen's Own Cameron Highlanders played "Scotland the Brave" as Eric appeared. The big crowd clapped rhythmically to the music as the runners lined up.

The two Americans, Fitch and Taylor, were in matching track suits. Eric was in a sweater and slacks, with the Edinburgh University crest on his chest. Up in the stand overlooking the starting line were the Prince of Wales, the full British Olympic Committee and the whole British track and field team, come to pay tribute to Eric.

Many of his teammates were convinced he was unbeatable and therefore would win the 400 meters, whatever the opposition. Harold wanted Eric to win, but he had seen the American Fitch break the world record, and Eric would have to break that record to beat Fitch. It was asking a lot of even a great runner like Eric.

The race was to be run on two bends with an exceptionally long back straight, not an easy course. The six finalists began to dig in their starting positions. Eric was on the outside, a difficult place. But he seemed as calm as ever at the start of a race. He shook hands with the other runners.

"Have a good race, everybody," he said with a smile. "Remember, I don't expect to see you again—until after the race."

Everybody laughed. The Americans didn't consider Eric a big threat. He was much more used to the 100 meter sprint than this longer distance; they would run him into the ground. The American coach had assured his runners that they had nothing to fear from Eric Liddell.

"He's a flyer. He'll die before the end." Jackson Scholtz was the only one to have doubts and he wasn't running in this race. "Liddell's got something to prove, something personal," he cautioned the two American finalists. "Something guys like the coach'll never understand in a million years."

The French starter told the runners to get ready. The tension immediately shot up. Eric took off his warm-up sweater and slacks. Suddenly a familiar figure trotted up the track. It was Jackson Scholtz. He handed Eric a folded paper and walked quickly away. Eric unfolded the paper and read: "In the Old Book, it says 'He that honors me, I will honor.' Good luck! Jackson Scholtz."

Eric felt as he had when Andy offered his place in the 400 meters. Perhaps it was more than a fine sporting gesture, perhaps it was the will of God. Visibly moved, Eric nodded his thanks to Scholtz, then concentrated on preparing for the race.

"Ready, gentlemen!" cried the French starter.

The loudspeaker blared out an appeal for silence. The noisy crowd quietened immediately and a strange, tense atmosphere settled over the stadium. Eric took one final glance at the stands and waved to Sandy McGrath. Then he noticed Jennie sitting beside his friend. His sister had travelled from Scotland to watch him in spite of her feelings about his running. He waved eagerly to her. She waved back, smiling broadly. Eric was grateful for this boost to his spirit. He felt as if this were a moment in his life when everything was right for his supreme offering to God.

Eric told himself, I must run the first 200 meters as hard as I can, and then for the second 200 meters, with God's help, I'll run even harder.

"To your marks. Set."

The starter held his pistol poised in the air and then the silence of the stadium was broken by a loud shot.

Eric took the lead immediately. He swept ahead of the other runners, well in front at the first bend. How could he possibly keep up that tremendous pace? Behind him came his fellow Briton, Butler, and then the two Americans, Fitch and Taylor. Butler soon began to tire, unable to keep up with Eric's incredible drive, and then the race was between Eric and the two Americans. They waited for Eric to crack, confident that he couldn't maintain such speed over the whole 400 meters, but Eric surged on like a man inspired, even increasing his lead.

A gasp of astonishment went up from the crowd when at the halfway mark, Eric was three yards ahead. Fitch and Taylor strained every nerve and muscle to overtake him, but Eric's head went back and his arms whirled higher with the intensity of his effort, and his pace quickened. Taylor could no longer keep up and stumbled. Fitch, the world record holder, was falling back, well beaten.

The race was like a fantastic dream, with the result seemingly inevitable from the start. Eric was ahead all the way. It was as if a spirit had entered his body, urging him on, giving him the strength and endurance to push himself to the peak of his power.

Running like a man oblivious of his surroundings, the Flying Scot was alone in his glory as he reached the tape in a new world record time of $47^3/_5$ seconds.

The whole crowd, the French just as much as the British, stood up and cheered Eric Liddell's remarkable win, the greatest performance of the Games so far. Eric's wild natural style and his overwhelming superiority over all the other runners astonished everyone. Yet Eric himself seemed totally unaware of the effect he had had. He trotted back along the track to help the injured American, Taylor, who had collapsed ten yards from the tape. Taylor was grateful for Eric's concern at the moment of his own triumph and warmly grasped his hand. Jackson Scholtz hurried over to congratulate Eric, but he couldn't find words to express his admiration for the great race he had witnessed, and he, too, ended simply by shaking Eric's hand.

Then across the track came Harold Abrahams and Eric went to meet him. The two great runners, who had now both won gold medals, greeted each other a little shyly, and yet there was now a bond between them. They had both come of age at the Olympics, winning against the world's finest competition and passing their supreme test with courage and dignity.

Harold told Sam later, "Liddell is a greater runner than I am. He ran from start to finish with an inspired and passionate intensity I have never seen before in a runner."

The British team carried Eric shoulder high to present him to the Prince of Wales. The Prince applauded and Eric smiled as he remembered their last meeting. All was forgiven now he had won.

Jennie waited off to the side until he came away from the Prince and made his way through the crowd toward her. Her eyes were brimming with happy tears as she regarded him—this great Olympic hero, who was also her brother.

No Eye Has Seen

But, as it is written,
"What no eye has seen, nor ear heard,
nor the heart of man conceived,
what God has prepared for those who love him,
God has revealed to us through the Spirit."
1 Corinthians 2:9

The ultimate in winning is knowing that you have not done it alone. In Eric's case he is aware that the Lord Jesus Christ has been within him, beside him, in front of him, surrounding him, throughout this race. God uses worldly means to perform spiritual transformations. Sandy McGrath, Mr. Liddell, and himself were all means to give God glory, honor, and praise.

As the six 400-meter finalists approach their starting position, it is apparent that Eric has drawn the most difficult lane in which to run. It is difficult because, due to the staggered start of the 400 meters, it will require that Eric run blindly, not knowing where his competitors are in relation to himself. But Eric addresses this as he has so many other obstacles, calmly encouraging the others in the race, then going out and running his own race. His own race consists of running the first two hundred meters as fast as he can, while totally trusting in the Lord's strength during the second half, head thrown back, looking heavenward.

Eric dominates the race from start to finish. At the firing of the gun, he courageously takes the lead and keeps it until he bursts through the finish line. He could easily have been intimidated by his American opponent and world record holder, Horatio M. M. Finch. Eric's running, however, is a mere extension of his life; it reflects his absolute trust in God to see him through to the end.

Eric's victory is an unimaginable accomplishment. He not only wins, but he sets a world record. His victory is so convincing that even Harold exclaims, "Liddell is a greater runner than I am."

To make his victory complete, Eric's sister, Jennie, is there to share his triumph. It is indeed a pleasure to please the Lord.

Questions for Reflection and Discussion

1. We see Eric Liddell as a man naturally at ease with himself. Much of his attitude can be attributed to his trust in God. What is trust in God? How do you attain trust in God?

2. We are not told how Eric prepared spiritually for his running career. How do you prepare yourself spiritually for everyday living? What kinds of quiet times do you have in Bible reading and prayer? Do you meet the Lord daily, first thing in the morning? Do you take one day out of the week or month to be alone with Him?

3. How do you handle obstacles such as those Eric faced? Are you confident in knowing God is with you? Do you peacefully and gracefully believe that He who has begun a good work in you will complete it?

4. Eric did not have any idea what the outcome of his years of training would be, yet he had faith in that which he did not yet see. What kind of faith do you have? Does it sustain you during your trials?

5. Do you remember to thank God for your accomplishments or do you honestly believe that you attain them by your own doing? Do you thank others who have helped you during your endeavors? When was the last time you thanked your parents for their help and love?

11

Harold Abrahams and Eric Liddell returned to Britain as national heroes, legends in their own time.

They were mobbed at Victoria Station when they reached London.

Sybil was there to welcome Harold home. She saw at once how changed he was. The tension, the aggression, the driving ambition were missing from his face. He had fulfilled his dream and he had become more relaxed, more tolerant, more *human*. It was as if he had grown up through his Olympic struggles and was now a man. He was impatient with all the hero worship. "Let's run away and get married," he told Sybil. And they did.

Eric returned to Scotland where he was carried through the streets of Edinburgh. He was equally impatient with his public role and soon left for China to pursue his missionary work with Jennie and his parents, far from the spotlight.

Their running days were over.

Soon after the Olympics, Harold Abrahams injured himself and retired from international running.

Eric Liddell remained in China and died in a Japanese prison camp close to the end of World War Two. All Scotland mourned the Flying Scot, whose wild natural running was beyond rational explanation but was never forgotten by anyone who saw it.

Harold lived on into old age. By the time he died in 1978, he was a leading sports writer and broadcaster and the Elder Statesman of British athletics, more established in society than he had ever imagined he would be when he first started out at Cambridge.

A memorial service was held in St. Mary's Church in the center of London to "honor the legend" of the great runner, and inevitably his name was linked with Eric Liddell's. The large congregation included Protestant ministers and Jewish rabbis, statesmen and great athletes, Jews and Christians alike, who had known Harold Abrahams or even run against him long ago.

"Let us now praise famous men and our fathers that begat us. All these men were honored in their generations. . . ."

The voice belonged to Lord Andrew Lindsay, an old man himself now. As he slowly recalled Harold Abrahams' great races of fifty years before, the past began to come alive again. The old men in the congregation were misty-eyed, remembering. How different the Olympics were in those days! So innocent and amateurish compared to the political arena the Olympics had become! Harold Abrahams and Eric Liddell were now eloquent reminders of the half-lost Olympic ideal.

Sitting in the front row, Aubrey Montague, an old man now, too, could almost see the young runners as they were in those golden days training for the 1924 Olympics, racing together in a pack along the beach, their feet pounding to a rhythm as steady as a drumbeat, as if they were performing a timeless ritual of human endeavor.

The church choir soared into the hymn that always reminded Aubrey of Harold and Eric:

"Bring me my bow of burning gold
Bring me my arrows of desire

"Bring me my spear, oh! Clouds unfold
Bring me my chariot of fire!

"I will not cease from mental fight
Nor shall my sword sleep in my hand."

The youthful voices conjuring up Blake's *Jerusalem* seemed to sing of the two great runners.

He could see their faces standing out in the pack, Harold with his look of intense concentration and Eric, his head back, his eyes turned up toward heaven.

Such men are immortal in their moments of glory, Aubrey thought. We need their memory to inspire us in our great race.

For after all life is a great race and what are we but runners.

Count It All Joy

Count it all joy, my brethren, when you meet various trials, for you know that the testing of your faith produces steadfastness. And let steadfastness have its full effect, that you may be perfect and complete, lacking in nothing.

James 1:2, 4, RSV

As this poignant story comes to a close, we see how Eric and Harold are united in their need to escape their hero worship. They have no need to revel in their past accomplishments, but rather a desire to move on, to keep going forward in life. Both men have tasted both victory and near defeat; they have experienced trials that they never imagined when they began their individual Olympic adventures. A bit of idealism that each held for the Olympics is dimmed. There is more to life than running, or even winning

144

gold medals. But it has been in the striving that Harold and Eric have matured, become wiser, and had their lives enriched.

These experiences of valleys and mountaintops prove invaluable to both of them. Harold now knows who he is and what he has accomplished. The fight is over — he has won his place in history and, more than that, his identity. Eric now can move on to his ultimate work in life, his missionary work in China. His experiences as an athlete will prove invaluable to his work as a missionary. His trust in God remains unwavering — even to giving up his life for the expressed purpose of telling others that Jesus lives, loves them, and desires to save them from eternal Hell.

Questions for Reflection and Discussion

1. How do you handle success? Do you glory in it and take the credit, or do you give glory to God? How do you give God the glory?
2. Our two heroes are content in winning and probably recognize that their struggles have matured them as men. Do you allow the struggles, the testing of your faith, to teach you endurance and a greater dependence on Jesus Christ? In what way do your trials solidify your relationship with God?
3. If life is a race, and you are a runner, how could you run your race more effectively for God? What specific changes would you make in your character and in your lifestyle?

Chariots of Fire

THE AWARD-WINNING MOVIE

Allied Stars presents an Enigma Production

Starring
   BEN CROSS
   IAN CHARLESON
   NIGEL HAVERS
   CHERYL CAMPBELL
   ALICE KRIGE

Guest Stars
   LINDSAY ANDERSON
   DENNIS CHRISTOPHER
   NIGEL DAVENPORT
   BRAD DAVIS
   PETER EGAN
   SIR JOHN GIELGUD
   IAN HOLM
   PATRICK MAGEE

Screenplay by
   COLIN WELLAND

Music by
   VANGELIS

146

Executive Producer
 DODI FAYED

Produced by
 DAVID PUTTNAM

Directed by
 HUGH HUDSON

A LADD COMPANY AND WARNER BROS. RELEASE